# MODERN MILITARY AIRCRAFT

# HORNET

## By Lou Drendel
## Color Illustrations by Lou Drendel

# squadron/signal publications

**ISBN 0-89747-204-7**

**If you have any photographs of the aircraft, armor, soldiers or ships of any
nation, particularly wartime snapshots, why not share them with us and help
make Squadron/Signal's books all the more interesting and complete in the
future. Any photograph sent to us will be copied and the original returned. The
donor will be fully credited for any photos used. Please send them to:**

Squadron/Signal Publications, Inc.
1115 Crowley Drive.
Carrollton, TX 75011-5010.

# Photo Credits

| | |
|---|---|
| U.S. Navy | McDonnell Douglas |
| Lou Drendel | Norman C Taylor |
| Northrop | Bryan Rogers |
| Douglas Remington | General Electric |
| Dave Mason | Mike 'Shooter' Shot |
| Tail Hook Photo Service/Robert L. Lawson | |

# INTRODUCTION

The F/A-18 Hornet is the best all-around fighter ever built. That is a strong statement, but one which can be supported by an examination of the Hornet's capabilities. How did the Hornet get to be the best fighter? And, why don't more people know that it is the best? The Hornet's path to its current operational position was circuitous, and at times torturous.

In appearance, the F/A-18 is remarkably similar to its oldest ancestor, the Northrop P-530 Cobra. The P-530 was designed in 1966 by Northrop's Vice President for advanced programs, Lee Begin. In spite of the fact that the P-530 was designed from the beginning to perform a multitude of missions, it was small compared to its most successful contemporary, the F-4 Phantom. The Cobra was projected to weigh in at 23,000 pounds gross weight, while the Phantom was double that. But it wasn't the Phantom that shunted the career of the P-530 on to the *going-nowhere* siding of fighter development. It was the equally large, powerful, and complex F-15 Eagle that occupied the developmental thinking of the USAF in the late 60's and early 70's, to the exclusion of almost all other fighter designs.

The idea of a small, simple fighter was not new to Northrop. Their adaptation of the T-38 Talon trainer into the F-5 Freedom Fighter was an international success even as the P-530 was being ignored by the Pentagon, which had not yet caught the lightweight fighter bug. There was another very successful international lightweight fighter whose popularity inspired Northrop to advance the idea of selling the P-530 as a collaborative venture with foreign governments. The Lockheed F-104 Starfighter had seen very limited service with USAF, but had become the mainstay of seven NATO air forces and Japan while being manufactured and/or assembled overseas. The F-5 had not achieved the popularity of the F-104 in 1966, but it was well on its way to surpassing the fast (and unforgiving) Starfighter in sales.

Northrop intended the P-530 to be yet another successful international fighter, and to that end they put together a presentation for the aviation press of Europe and Australia in January of 1971. Their full-scale mockup, complete with Dutch markings, was displayed at the 1973 Paris air show. In spite of the best efforts of Northrop's salesmen in trumpeting the advanced features of the P-530, no orders were forthcoming. While no foreign orders seemed imminent, the possibilities for an American order improved when a coterie of hard-core fighter proponents in the Pentagon finally made an impression with their efforts to procure a lightweight fighter for the United States.

The request for proposals for a lightweight fighter was answered by Boeing, General Dynamics, Lockheed, and Northrop. The two finalists chosen for prototype procurement were the General Dynamics F-16 and the Northrop F-17.

The first of two YF-17 prototypes was rolled out on 4 April, 1974. Northrop claimed that its latest in a long line of lightweight performers (T-38, F-5A, F-5B, and F-5E) would outmaneuver any operational aircraft known. At the time of the YF-17 rollout, Northrop had produced over 2,000 of the T-38/F-5 series. That record, coupled with impressive technological advancements, seemed reason enough to be optimistic about their upcoming head-to-head competition with the General Dynamics YF-16. The USAF had established a flyaway cost goal of $3 million per airplane, in fiscal 1972 dollars, if 100 fighters per year were produced for three years. Northrop had spent eight years and millions of dollars in company funds to develop the advanced technological features of the YF-17. With 1.6 million man hours and 10,000 hours of wind tunnel testing behind it, the YF-17 was an impressive candidate.

While the airframe of the YF-17 contained innovative aerodynamic features as well as the new graphite composites and a cockpit designed for ease of operation, one of the most impressive things about the new fighter was its engines. The General Electric YJ-101 measured only 145 inches in length and 32 inches in diameter. It produced 15,000 pounds of thrust in afterburner, which gave it a thrust-to-weight ratio of 8 to 1. The two YJ-101s of the YF-17 gave the YF-17 a projected top speed in the Mach 2 class. Compared to the J-79 which powered the F-4 Phantom, the YJ-101 was one third shorter, half the weight, had 40% fewer parts, eight fewer rotating stages, and almost twice the thrust-to-weight ratio. For an engine with such impressive performance gains, it was remarkably trouble-free, completing USAF/Prototype Preliminary Flight Rating Tests in just 18 months and 1,200 hours of ground test running.

Northrop Chief Test Pilot Hank Chouteau made the first flight of the YF-17 on 9 June 1974 from Edwards AFB, California. The 61 minute flight was trouble-free and the YF-17 reached a top speed of 610 mph at 18,000 feet. On two subsequent flights Chouteau accelerated to Mach 1 at 30,000 feet without the use of afterburner. Northrop claimed that this was the first aircraft to fly supersonic without afterburner. The pilot for the fourth test flight was USAF Lt. Col. Jim Rider, commander of the Lightweight Fighter Joint Test Force at Edwards AFB.

By the time those first flights were made, the YF-17 had been under development for eight years. Northrop had used their successful F-5 design as a basis for developing a follow-on air combat fighter, feeling all along that high performance and combat capability could be embodied in a smaller airplane than the F-4, F-14, or F-15. But even though many new features were incorporated in the design, it was never thought of as a technology demonstrator. It was designed from the outset to be an operational airplane.

Northrop's design studies had determined that maneuverability in the transonic speed range was most important in an air combat fighter. High Mach numbers were not necessarily the best measure of an effective fighter. Turn rate was. Wing loading and radius of turn went out the window. What mattered was how fast you could change heading...how quickly you could bring your guns to bear on the other guy. And that called for exceptional energy management capability; climb, acceleration, and turn rate became the standards by which Northrop measured their developmental efforts.

**The keynote speaker at the unveiling ceremony of the first of two YF-17 prototypes, on 4 April 1974, was Secretary of the Air Force John L. McLucas. Billed as a 'technology demonstrator', the YF-17 was one of two finalists in the USAF lightweight fighter competition, ultimately won by the General Dynamics YF-16. (Northrop)**

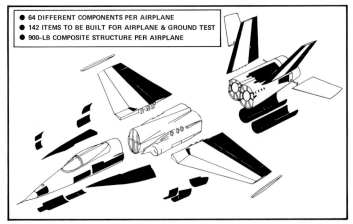

● 64 DIFFERENT COMPONENTS PER AIRPLANE
● 142 ITEMS TO BE BUILT FOR AIRPLANE & GROUND TEST
● 900-LB COMPOSITE STRUCTURE PER AIRPLANE

In order to accomplish those design objectives, it was necessary to venture pretty far afield from established design criteria. Though the YF-17 and its successor, the F-18, don't seem radically different in appearance from other contemporary fighters, the YF-17 was unusual for its day.

High angle of attack maneuvers are de rigueur for air combat maneuvering, and in order to improve the YF-17's characteristics in this regime, large, highly swept leading edge extensions were added to a wing which was basically straight, with a broad chord at the tip. The leading edge extensions ran all the way out to the front of the cockpit, adding stability in high angles of attack. The engine intakes were buried under the wing at the leading edge of the main span. This position limited the length of the ducts, which reduced weight and drag, and improved inlet performance in high AOA maneuvers. Automatically programmed leading and trailing edge flaps added to the YF-17's maneuverability. They were programmed to extend as a function of angle-of-attack and Mach number. The leading edge flaps would extend up to 25 degrees, while the trailing edge flaps would extend up to 20 degrees during air combat maneuvering. The pilot could manually override the automatic controls.

Twin vertical tails were necessary to offset the vortex flows off of the leading edge extensions of the wings. The twin tails are mounted far forward to close the aerodynamic gap between the trailing edge of the wing and the leading edge of the vertical tail. This results in a smooth and drag free fuselage airflow. The forward position of the tails eliminated airflow interference around the engine nozzles, and saved weight by eliminating the need for any major rear fuselage carry through structure.

The large horizontal stabilizer provided very effective pitch changes with a minimum of deflection. It also served as the primary roll control at high Mach numbers. Left and right stabilizers deflected differentially up to 3 degrees throughout the entire YF-17 speed range. At the lowest maneuvering speeds, the ailerons provided 90%

**One of the innovative features of the YF-17 was the use of graphite composites. Some thirty percent lighter than aluminum, with twice the tensile strength of steel, graphite composites contributed to the ultimate success of the Northrop design. (Northrop)**

of the roll control, while at the highest speeds, the single-loop fly-by-wire ailerons were programmed out of the roll control completely. 900 pounds of graphite composites replaced what would have been 1200 pounds of aluminum in various parts of the YF-17's basic structure.

The cockpit featured a single throttle grip for both engines, with dual couplings to the engine fuel control linkages. (In an engine-out situation, the pilot could disengage the linkage to that engine without removing his hand from the throttle.) The throttle grip also contained several other switches, including speed brakes and radar controls. The control stick was left in the conventional center position to allow the pilot to fly with either hand. The rudder pedals were raised 5 inches, and the seat reclined to give leg support for this position, which increased pilot G tolerance by 1 G. The glass instrument panel of the F/A-18 was one of the few visionary features not included in the YF-17, which had conventional round gauges.

The flight test program for the YF-17 was designed to be completed in a year, but was shortened because of pressure from Europe. The lightweight fighter program eventually evolved into the air combat fighter program which would supply at least four NATO countries with a replacement for their F-104s. These countries were anxious to make a decision on a new fighter, and the source selection date was moved up to January of 1975. Using inflight refueling provided by several Air National Guard tanker units, the YF-17 test force managed to compress a year of testing into six months. It was a bitter disappointment when USAF picked the F-16 as its ACF in January of 1975.

The main reasons were range and cost, both a result of the F-16's Pratt & Whitney F-100 engine. Since it was the same engine used in the F-15, developmental costs for the F-16 engine were near zero, and maintainability would be simplified with both of the Air Force's primary fighters using the same engine. Range was extended because of the F-100's high by-pass fan. (The engines in the YF-17 were turbojets.) Finally, General Dynamics was able to convince the Air Force that there was no significant advantage to twin engines, especially since the newer engines were proving more and more reliable. Though the formal announcement of the NATO choice was not made until June of the following year, during the Paris Air Show, the USAF choice of the F-16 inspired serious price negotiations by the Europeans for the General Dynamics fighter. It was becoming evident that the only hope Northrop had of selling the F-17 was the U.S. Navy, which was in the market for a fighter to replace its Phantoms and Corsair IIs.

Congress had mandated that the Navy Air Combat Fighter (NACF) would be a navalized version of one of the finalists in the Air Force competition. They may have thought they were assuring that only one fighter would be produced for both Navy and Air Force, ala the F-4 Phantom, and in fact, that is what the general opinion was even after the F-16 was chosen. The wording of their mandate left room for doubt. As it was finally interpreted, the Navy choice was limited to either the Northrop or General Dynamics design. In practice it was stretched even further with the inclusion of yet another major defense contractor. Northrop had no recent experience in dealing with the U.S. Navy aircraft acquisition bureaucracy, and so were quick to accept an offer from McDonnell Douglas to collaborate on the NACF.

The YF-17 prototype dressed up for its F-18 sales role in front of the McDonnell Douglas headquarters hangar in St. Louis. The prototype carried an attractive Blue and White finish with Gold trim. (McDonnell Douglas)

McDonnell Douglas was one of the most experienced recent Naval Aircraft contractors at that time, and it had studied the F-16 and F-17 carefully to determine which of the two would be the best NACF candidate. They came to the conclusion that the Northrop fighter was the best choice for a carrier-based fighter. (A view not shared by LTV, which submitted a navalized F-16 for consideration. Of course, LTV was literally across the street from General Dynamics, making their collaboration a natural.) For its part, Northrop was happy to have McDonnell Douglas as a partner on the F-18. Northrop felt that the most lucrative contracts would come from foreign sales, an area that they were very knowledgeable in due to their F-5 programs. As a consequence, they allowed McDonnell Douglas to become the prime contractor for the F/A-18 for the U.S. Navy, while they staked out their claim on the F-18L. ('L' standing for land-based version.) Northrop expected the F-18L to be the export version of the F-18. They further expected it to account for far more sales than the U.S. Navy contract would generate.

Within four months of the USAF announcement that they had chosen the F-16 for their Air Combat Fighter (ACF), the Navy announced that its choice was the F-18. The European consortium had still not made a decision, and their task was further complicated by the inclusion of the F-18 in the equation. The Department of Defense made it clear that both should be considered when Secretary of Defense James Schlesinger informed U.S. embassies in NATO consortium countries of the Navy decision. He added that the F-18 would be available about 24 months later than the F-16, and that it would cost 20% more, be 23% heavier, have a 38% greater internal fuel capacity, 18% greater wing area, and a clean take-off weight 24% greater than the F-16. It was also thought that the F-18 avionics would be more suitable for the usually crummy European weather. Schlesinger's attempts to promote the F-18 came to nought. The Europeans finally selected the F-16.

It is obvious from looking at the foregoing figures that the F-18 had grown from the lightweight F-17 which had spawned it. While McDonnell Douglas kept the basic aerodynamic shape of the F-17, major design changes really created a whole new airplane in the F-18. These changes included: An enlarged nose to accommodate the 28 inch radar dish necessary for the Navy's weapons system search range requirement of over 30 nautical miles (the less stringent Air Force requirement could be accommodated with a 23 inch dish.) The addition of 50 square feet of wing area (from 350 to 400 square feet), with increases in both span and chord needed to accomplish this change. The aft fuselage width was increased by 4 inches and the engines were canted outward at the front in order to provide for more internal fuel capacity. The fuselage was stretched 5 inches, also to provide more fuel capacity. Advanced versions of the YJ-101 engines, designated F404-GE-400, were installed, providing an increase in thrust to 16,000 pounds per engine. The new engines also had a higher bypass flow ratio, which reduced specific fuel consumption. Some aerodynamic changes were made to improve low speed handling characteristics, including a 6 square foot increase in the area of the leading edge extensions. The maximum extension angle of the leading edge flaps was increased from 25 degrees to 35 degrees, and the trailing edge flap extension limit went from 20 to 45 degrees. This enabled the F-18, which was projected to weigh in over 6,000 pounds heavier than the F-17, to get down to the required carrier approach speed.

Landing on a carrier is a demanding task, and one of the most rigid requirements for carrier aircraft is rapid transition from descent at idle engine thrust to a positive rate of climb at maximum power. This is necessary because each landing on the angled deck is made with the idea that it is going to be a 'touch and go'. As the air-

**With the Northrop-McDonnell Douglas partnership solidified, the YF-17 became the F-18 prototype for worldwide sales demonstrations. Northrop still had hopes of using the 'Cobra' name, as evidenced by the Cobra painted on the nose. (via Norm Taylor)**

craft slams on to the deck, the pilot advances his throttle(s) to full power...just in case he misses the arresting gear with his hook. This is called a 'bolter' and if it happens, you had better have plenty of thrust if you want to avoid dribbling off the end of the angled deck for an expensive and possibly fatal splash.

To achieve a more rapid transition, the engineers at McDonnell and Northrop concentrated on improving lift characteristics. They did this by incorporating drooped shrouds under each wing. The shrouds are mounted along the leading edge of the flaps, and are flush with the top surface of each wing when the flaps are retracted. When the flaps are deployed, they droop downward slightly before pivoting out into the airstream below the wing. They pivot downward, forcing air flowing under the wing to conform more closely to each flap airfoil, preventing the separation that leads to stall. The ailerons were also drooped a full 45 degrees when flaps are deployed, which gave the F-18 full span flaps. (The ailerons continue to deflect differentially even in their drooped position to provide roll control.) Overall combat agility was enhanced with addition of a maneuvering flap system similar to that used on the F-5.

Assuming full production of the F-18, Northrop expected to have a 30% share of development engineering, and 40% of production. McDonnell was to be responsible for production of the forward fuselage, including all systems, wings, and landing gear, while Northrop built the rear fuselage, including engine installation. Final assembly would be at McDonnell Aircraft Company in St. Louis.

In September of 1975, Representative Dale Milford (D-Tex), testified before the tactical air subcommittee of the Senate Armed Services Committee. Though LTV was in his congressional district, Congressman Milford stated that his threat to sue the Navy for choosing the F-18 over the navalized F-16 was only motivated by a desire to acquire the best fighter for the Navy. Milford also threatened to sponsor a

contempt of congress resolution, citing the Navy for its failure to live up to the intent of the congressional mandate to choose the same fighter as the Air Force. The Navy replied that the wording to the congressional resolution gave them the option to choose between the F-16 and F-17, and that the F-18 was superior in at least twelve areas of comparison with the three LTV-presented versions of navalized F-16s. The Navy research specialists testified that they felt the F-18 was the best aircraft they could acquire, based upon current technology. The Navy's defense of its F-18 procurement decision was so well presented that Milford's protestations were generally interpreted as sour grapes and the navalized version of the F-16 never got beyond the drawing board.

During all of the design and evaluation work, the Navy/Marine Corps plan had been to acquire 800 Hornets with an ever-changing mix of fighter (F) versions, and attack (A) versions. It was thought that dedicating an aircraft to a specific mission would enable it to perform that mission more effectively. Since the airframe/engine package would not change, this meant that the specific tailoring of the aircraft for these missions would revolve around avionics. Advances in avionics and cockpit design narrowed the design differences to a point where the two merged, and by the time the Hornet rolled out of the McDonnell plant in September 1978 it had become the F/A-18, a much more versatile and potent package than had been envisioned in 1975.

The first flight of the Hornet took place on 18 November 1978. McDonnell Aircraft Company chief test pilot Jack Krings made the first takeoff in military power, using about 2,000 feet of runway. The fifty minute first flight was observed from an F-15 chase plane piloted by William H. Brinks. It was also recorded via telemetry downlinks. Krings was pleasantly surprised by the inherent stability

of the F-18, a feature not generally found in high performance fighters. The Hornet performed flawlessly throughout a battery of handling tests and Krings reported that it was "extremely stable" during approach, a most desirable feature in a carrier airplane. It was an auspicious beginning to the flight test program. Unfortunately, there were clouds on the Hornet's horizon which had nothing to do with the performance of the new fighter.

Under the terms of their partnership agreement with McDonnell Douglas, Northrop was to be awarded 30% of development work and 40% of production work for the carrier-based version of the F-18. The land-based version, which was basically the same airplane, but with several modifications, was to be Northrop's, with McDonnell assuming the sub-contractor role played by Northrop on the Navy version. When several foreign countries expressed interest in the production F-18, McDonnell began a sales effort. Canada was the first customer in line, and the Canadians wanted a piece of that production pie as a quid pro quo to signing a contract.

In October of 1979 Northrop filed suit against McDonnell, alleging that McDonnell had offered to divert Northrop work on export versions of the carrier-based F-18 to the customer as a condition of the sale. According to their suit, "McDonnell Douglas Corp has made these offers to divert Northrop work unilaterally and without consultation with Northrop, despite Northrop's express objections". Northrop also alleged that McDonnell was attempting to sell Israel a version of the F-18 which was substantially different than the Navy version, while Northrop was also attempting to interest Israel in its F-18L version of the Hornet. Northrop asked for an injunction against McDonnell's

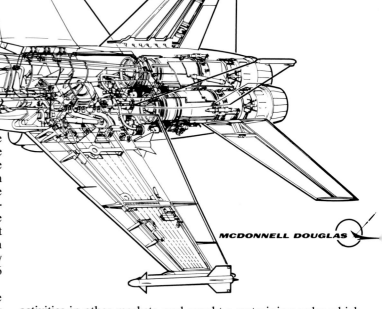

activities in other markets, and sought a restraining order which would prevent McDonnell from offering to sell or produce for any foreign government F-18 aircraft, or any other derivatives of Northrop's YF-17 that were not carrier-suitable; offering to sell to or produce any foreign customer F-18 aircraft or any other derivatives of the YF-17 on terms that were not consistent with the basic licensing agreement; offering to any party other than Northrop Corp. any work, production effort, task, role or responsibility of any kind or character, to which Northrop Corp. is entitled under the basic licensing agreement; soliciting any offers, bids or proposals from any party other than Northrop Corp. to provide, supply, produce or furnish any work, production effort, task, role or responsibility of any kind or character to which Northrop Corp is entitled under basic license agreement and the Navy subcontract.

The two partners had suddenly become adversaries, and an amended lawsuit by Northrop sought $400 million in damages from McDonnell, while a counter-suit by McDonnell sought $100 million

The first F/A-18 prototype was rolled out of the factory, sans paint, for a brief photo session on the empty McDonnell Douglas ramp on 21 July 1978. (McDonnell Douglas via Norman E. Taylor)

from Northrop. A preliminary hearing resulted in denial of Northrop's request for an injunction. While they were at odds over the handling of foreign sales, both aerospace giants realized that sales efforts should not be impeded by their legal battles, and they reached an agreement whereby the Canadian sales effort could continue.

The legal battle dragged on for six years, and was not settled until the Navy refused to pay legal costs charged to the F-18 program overhead by both companies. On 8 April 1985 McDonnell Douglas and Northrop announced that they had resolved all contractual disputes. The terms of the settlement called for McDonnell to pay Northrop $50 million. McDonnell Douglas and Northrop entered into a new contract arrangement which specified that McDonnell would be prime contractor for all F-18 variants, including land-based versions, and that Northrop would be the principle subcontractor. McDonnell would be licensor for any licensed production. McDonnell stated that the $50 million would be paid promptly, and that the payment would have no adverse effect on company earnings for 1985.

The flight test program began in early 1979 at Naval Air Test Center (NATC), Patuxent River, Maryland. It was a highly visible test program from beginning to end, but one which allowed the Hornet to silence most defense critics with its outstanding performance. The command augmentation program delighted test pilots with the smooth ride it provided at low level in turbulent air. While F-4 chase planes were bouncing all over the sky, the F/A-18 was as steady as a rock, making for a very good weapons delivery platform. The Hornet's agility was fast becoming legend as it repeatedly 'lost' chase planes that were supposed to be monitoring its maneuvers.

The Hornet's performance was not the only thing that was making the Navy happy. The Hornet's maintainability was better than anyone had hoped for. The Navy planning standard was eighteen man hours of maintenance (MMH) for every flight hour (FH). The A-7, which was the last attack airplane to enter the Navy inventory, had a MMH/FH ratio of 24, and the F-4 Phantom's ratio was even

higher. The Hornet MMH/FH during the first six months of the test program was eleven!

A total of eleven F/A-18 prototypes were built for the flight test program. The second aircraft made its first flight in March of 1979, and the last made its first flight in March of 1981. Until the F-18, the usual method of flight testing was to base prototypes at or near the manufacturer of major systems, (avionics, engine, airframe) so that testing on those systems could be closely monitored by the manufacturer. The Hornet employed a new test system, called 'Principal Site Concept', where all prototypes were based at one location and all flight testing was under direct control of the Navy.

Since the F-18 was aerodynamically so close to the YF-17, no surprises were expected in that area, and the flight test program was expected to proceed rapidly and smoothly. It did go rapidly, but not quite as smoothly as the Navy would have liked. The Principal Site Concept enabled the Navy to identify problems more quickly and work on their solution. This made for a quick flight test program, but one which seemed to generate a lot of negative publicity, just because it was compressed. As early as the summer of 1979 two serious problems had been identified and solutions were incorporated. A higher than acceptable nose wheel liftoff speed was corrected by filling in the snag in the horizontal stabilator which gave the stabilator more authority earlier, and by toeing in the rudders on takeoff. A further change was made to flight control software which reprogrammed the leading edge flaps, reducing takeoff and approach speeds even more. The stabilator snag had been incorporated to correct flutter, so that became a concern. Cooling of the cockpit and avionics bay was taking too much fuel, severely limiting the F-18's range. As the fine-tuning of these systems narrowed the acceptable temperature range, that problem was gradually solved. Also by the summer of 1979, the total buy of F-18s had been raised to a projected 1,366 aircraft.

From 30 October to 3 November 1979 the number three Hornet was used to conduct initial sea trials aboard USS AMERICA off the Virginia Capes. A total of seventeen touch-and-go landings and thirty-two arrested landings and takeoffs were made by two Navy test pilots during eight flights which covered fourteen hours. The aircraft met all expectations, and achieved 100% availability during the test period. Ironically, it was damaged upon completion of the tests when it veered off the runway at NAS Oceana and collapsed the nose gear.

Another aerodynamic problem encountered was high wing loading of the outer wing, which reduced the roll rate and degraded performance. The leading edge of the wing outboard of the wing fold joint could be seen to curl up when pulling Gs. The solution to that problem was to remove the snag which had been designed into the leading edge of the wing for structural purposes. Slots in the leading edge extensions, which had been designed into the YF-17 in order to direct the airflow to the engine inlets, were removed to reduce drag and increase range and endurance. The radius of the leading edge of the wings was increased by rounding off the leading edge. This pro-

The differences in size and shape between the YF-17 (left) and F/A-18 (right) are evident in this family portrait of the number three Hornet prototype and the YF-17 at Edwards AFB. (McDonnell Douglas via Norm Taylor)

The number one Hornet prototype on its first flight in November of 1978. The fully extended landing gear when compared to its position on the ground gives a good indication of the shock absorbing capability of the gear. (McDonnell Douglas via Norm Taylor)

vided a 5% increase in range during sub-sonic cruise. The exhaust for the environmental control system was fitted with a fairing which redirected the exhaust to the rear, instead of 90 degrees to the air stream as it had been in the original design.

The General Electric F404 engines achieved consistent high marks throughout the flight test program. Early in the program, test pilots discovered that they were able to ram the throttles forward from flight idle into full afterburner, then go back to flight idle just as quickly, without causing a compressor stall. Maximum speeds generated early in the test program were Mach 1.6 at 40,000 feet and Mach 1.5 at 50,000 feet. Full stick rolls were made at 40,000 feet at 115 knots, with less than 3 degrees of sideslip. It was becoming apparent that the Hornet would not break any speed records, but that it would be an unbeatable foe in a turning fight.

The weapons system performed nearly flawlessly from the beginning. The first firing of an AIM-7 Sparrow resulted in a direct hit on a BQM-34 target drone, and the first Sidewinder firing achieved the planned 2.5 foot miss of a target drone. The 20MM gun was test fired in both 4,000 and 6,000 rounds per minute modes in a continuous burst on the ground, and was fired in the air while the radar was in the search and tracking modes.

In spite of the success of the test program, costs were accelerating on the F/A-18 program to the point where many Congressmen were questioning the wisdom of continuing with procurement. By March of 1980, the overall program cost for acquisition of 1,366 airplanes had reached an estimated $34 billion. This was close to the projected cost of the MX missile program, and prompted Congress to compare the two programs in terms of their value to the defense of the nation. And it wasn't only Congress that was wondering about the cost of the Hornet.

On at least two occasions in 1979-80, the Navy had examined termination of the program in favor of procurement of additional F-14 Tomcats and extension of the service life of their A-7s. The F-18, progeny of the 'cheap' lightweight fighter, had grown in cost and complexity to the point where the individual airplane cost was within a couple of million dollars of the F-14 Tomcat...the most expensive fighter the Navy had ever bought! Those in the Navy...and there were many...who favored more F-14s, continued to press the issue of accelerating costs of the F-18 program.

Armed with its primary air-to-air weapons load of two AIM-7 Sparrow missiles on the fuselage and two AIM-9 Sidewinders on the wingtips, the number one Hornet prototype conducts a test flight to test the maneuvering flap system. (McDonnell Douglas)

The first Hornet was painted in White and Blue with Gold trim. 50% of its airframe structure is aluminum, 17% steel, 12% titanium, 10% carbon/expoxy composites, and 10% other miscellaneous materials. (McDonnell Douglas)

(Left) The number one Hornet prototype demonstrates the use of the rear fuselage speed brake. The speed brake well is painted in Red. (McDonnell Douglas)

8

(Above) Bureau Number 160781 was the first two seat Hornet prototype. In addition to testing the two seat configuration, it was used to conduct armament separation tests of the AIM-7 and AIM-9 missiles. (McDonnell Douglas via Norm Taylor)

(Below) The F/A-18 car carry an impressive variety of weapons on nine external stores stations in addition to the 20MM M-61 Vulcan cannon carried internally in the nose. (McDonnell Douglas)

(Above) The first three F/A-18 prototypes on the flight line at Naval Air Test Center (NATC), NAS Patuxent River, Maryland parked alongside the other McDonnell Douglas Marine Corps tactical aircraft, the AV-8 Harrier. (McDonnell Douglas)

(Below) T-1, the first F/A-18B, on an early test flight armed with Sparrow and Sidewinder air-to-air missiles. (McDonnell Douglas)

9

The third single-seat Hornet prototype (BuNo 160777) was used to test the carrier suitability of the Hornet. Field arrested landings were carried out at Pax River prior to sea trials. (McDonnell Douglas)

In early 1980 the economic policies of the Carter Administration were coming home to roost in the form of double-digit inflation and interest rates which would have made a Loan Shark blush. The F-18 program suffered from both, as did all defense programs. Nevertheless, serious consideration of cancellation of the F-18 program was made within the Executive Branch. The Office of Management and Budget (OMB) conducted a study which indicated that procuring F-14s, A-7s, and AV-8B Harriers in similar numbers to the planned buy of 1,366 F/A-18s would be more cost-effective. And finally, it was an election year. The election of 1980 was seen as a mandate for increased defense spending, as the Carter Administration and several left-wing democratic senators were swept from office in one of the biggest landslide victories ever posted in a presidential election.

There were two crashes during the flight test program. The first came on 8 September 1980 when McDonnell Chief Test Pilot Jack Krings, along with backseater Marine Lt. Col. Gary Post, were ferrying the number two TF/A-18 from England, where it had performed during the Farnborough Air Show, to Spain for demonstrations. They experienced catastrophic right engine failure shortly after departure from Farnborough and attempted to land at RAF Boscombe Down. The right low pressure turbine disc had failed, causing damage to the flight control system that eventually led to loss of control of the aircraft, forcing the two men to eject at 4,000 feet and over 400 knots. Both received injuries in the form of broken bones.

The second crash occurred at NAS Pax River during high AOA

**The second series of sea trials for the number three Hornet prototype were conducted aboard the nuclear carrier USS CARL VINSON during May of 1982. (McDonnell Douglas via Norm Taylor)**

The number three prototype arrives over USS AMERICA prior to making its first carrier landing. LCDR Dick Richards and Lt Ken Grubbs made thirty-two landings and catapult launches during three days of trials conducted in October of 1979. (McDonnell Douglas)

testing. Lt C.T. Brannon, a VX-4 test pilot, achieved a previously unseen condition which resulted in a flat spin. He spun down to 5,000 feet from 20,000 feet without being able to recover. Brannon then ejected and the number twelve F-18 crashed in 15 feet of water in the Chesapeake Bay, from which the parts were recovered. Two subsequent test flights were able to duplicate this condition (though it took over 100 attempts to do it) and recovery methods were noted. On the first, the contractor pilot reduced power on the outboard engine to idle, while advancing the inboard engine to full afterburner. On the second, the flight control computer was shut down to allow full aileron deflection.

The first production example of the F/A-18 Hornet was delivered in May of 1980, and the first Fleet Readiness Squadron (VFA-125) was commissioned at NAS Lemoore in November of 1980.

(Above) The pilot makes pre-flight checks of the Hornet's built in test features prior to beginning the day's trials aboard USS CARL VINSON during May of 1982. (McDonnell Douglas via Norm Taylor)

(Left) LCDR Ken Grubbs taxies out of the arresting gear aboard VINSON after an arrested landing. The four degree glideslope of the Hornet gives the pilot a better view of the deck on approach and the reliable excess power of the General Electric engines allows a safe waveoff at intermediate power — even on one engine! (McDonnell Douglas)

Full span leading and trailing edge flaps are used to lower the Hornet's approach speed to 134 knots, the required approach speed necessary for a safe carrier landing. (McDonnell Douglas via Norm Taylor)

The number four Hornet (BuNo 160778) was used to test the structural integrity of the design, pulling up to 11.25 Gs during one symmetrical pull out and 9 Gs in a rolling pull out. (McDonnell Douglas)

The Number four prototype armed with four Mk 84 low drag bombs. The Hornet can deliver conventional ordnance with almost three times the accuracy of the A-7 Corsair II. (McDonnell Douglas)

The 2,000 pound MK-84 low drag bomb is used to attack hardened positions. The weapons delivery system in the F/A-18 allows consistently high bombing scores to be achieved. (McDonnell Douglas via Norm Taylor)

The number four prototype was also used to test and verify the Hornets aerial refueling system. Tests were conducted using the KA-3B Skywarrior tanker from NATC. (McDonnell Douglas via Norm Taylor)

(Above) The number seven single-seat prototype (BuNo 160782) fires an AIM-9 Sidewinder from the outboard pylon. The outboard pylon can mount two Sidewinders on a dual launcher rail, giving the F/A-18 a total missile armament of six AIM-9s and two AIM-7 Sparrows. (McDonnell Douglas)

(Below) The number seven prototype flies formation with its Marine Corps predecessor, the F-4J Phantom II. The three cameras mounted on the wingtip were used to photograph Sparrow missile launches from the fuselage station. (McDonnell Douglas)

(Right) Navy Squadron VX-5, based at NAS China Lake conducted tests of the Hornets weapons systems, using standard fleet tactics. This F/A-18 of VX-5 is about to be launched from USS CONSTELLATION (CV-64) armed with MK-82 low drag bombs on the outboard and centerline pylons. (McDonnell Douglas)

(Below) An F/A-18 of VX-5 on the port catapult of USS CONSTELLATION. VX-5 flew a series of tests designed to test the aircraft and its systems in a tactical shipboard situation. (McDonnell Douglas)

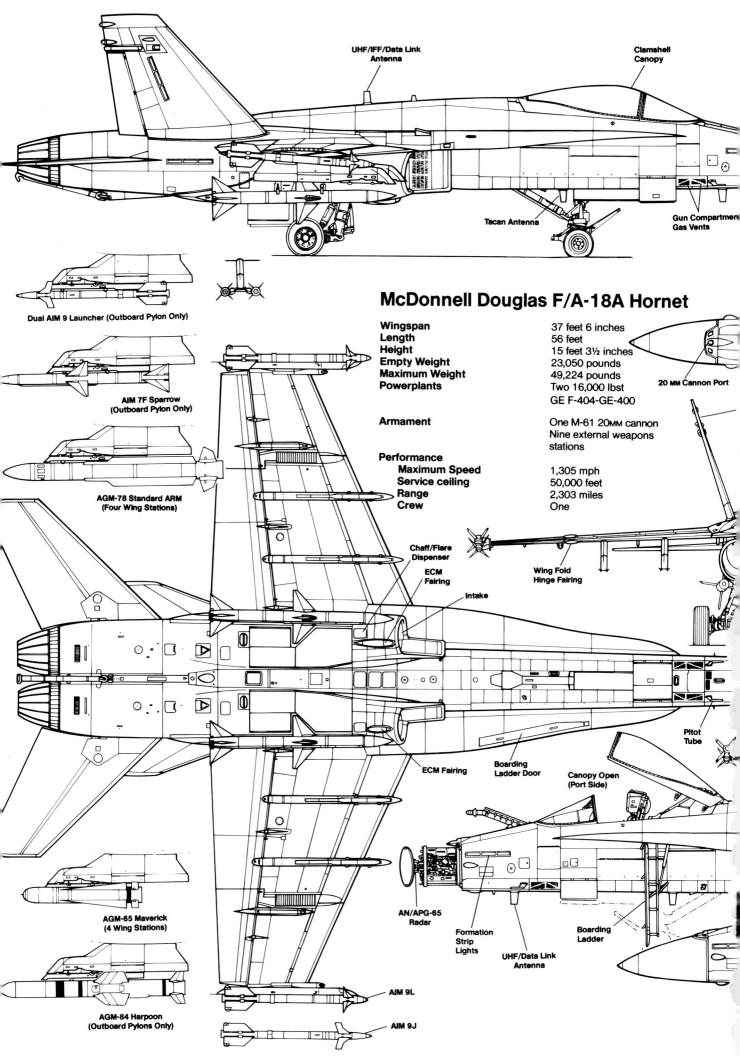

UHF/IFF/Data Link
Antenna

Clamshell
Canopy

Tacan Antenna

Gun Compartment
Gas Vents

Dual AIM 9 Launcher (Outboard Pylon Only)

AIM 7F Sparrow
(Outboard Pylon Only)

AGM-78 Standard ARM
(Four Wing Stations)

# McDonnell Douglas F/A-18A Hornet

| | |
|---|---|
| Wingspan | 37 feet 6 inches |
| Length | 56 feet |
| Height | 15 feet 3½ inches |
| Empty Weight | 23,050 pounds |
| Maximum Weight | 49,224 pounds |
| Powerplants | Two 16,000 lbst GE F-404-GE-400 |
| Armament | One M-61 20mm cannon Nine external weapons stations |
| Performance | |
| Maximum Speed | 1,305 mph |
| Service ceiling | 50,000 feet |
| Range | 2,303 miles |
| Crew | One |

20 MM Cannon Port

Chaff/Flare
Dispenser

ECM
Fairing

Intake

Wing Fold
Hinge Fairing

ECM Fairing

Boarding
Ladder Door

Pitot
Tube

Canopy Open
(Port Side)

AN/APG-65
Radar

Formation
Strip
Lights

UHF/Data Link
Antenna

Boarding
Ladder

AGM-65 Maverick
(4 Wing Stations)

AGM-84 Harpoon
(Outboard Pylons Only)

AIM 9L

AIM 9J

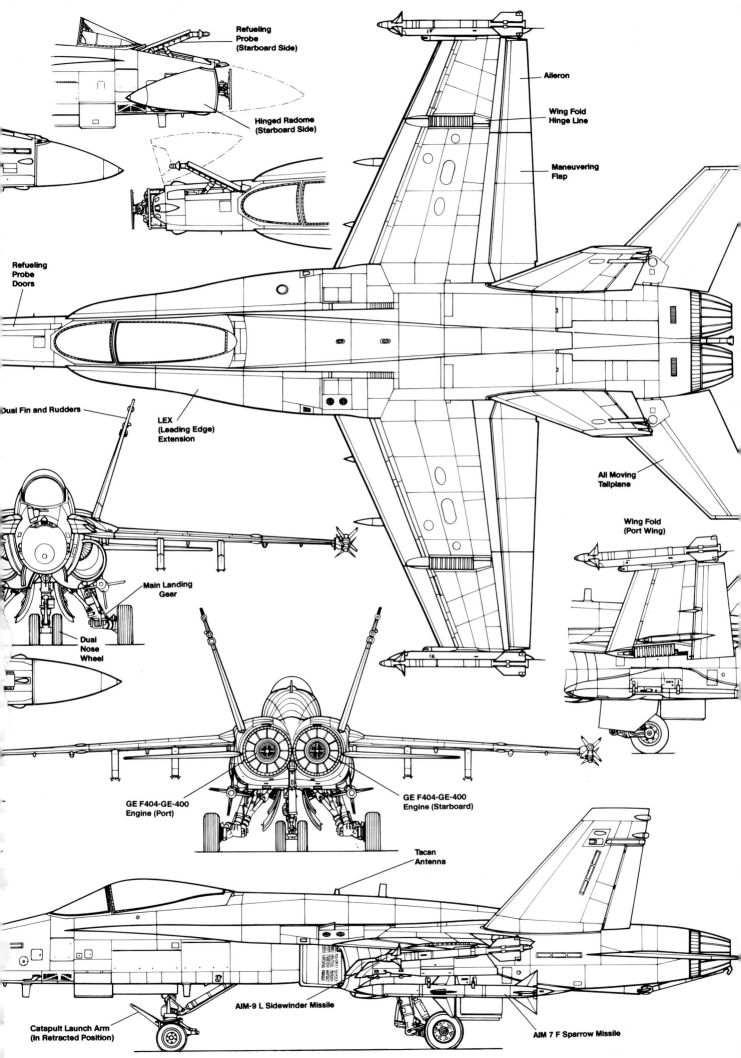

Refueling
Probe
(Starboard Side)

Hinged Radome
(Starboard Side)

Aileron

Wing Fold
Hinge Line

Maneuvering
Flap

Refueling
Probe
Doors

Dual Fin and Rudders

LEX
(Leading Edge)
Extension

All Moving
Tailplane

Wing Fold
(Port Wing)

Main Landing
Gear

Dual
Nose
Wheel

GE F404-GE-400
Engine (Port)

GE F404-GE-400
Engine (Starboard)

Tacan
Antenna

Catapult Launch Arm
(In Retracted Position)

AIM-9 L Sidewinder Missile

AIM 7 F Sparrow Missile

The number five prototype (BuNo 160779) was the first F/A-18 to have the full avionics/weapons system installed. The radar had previously been test flown in a T-39. Number five carries the same White and Blue with Gold trim paint scheme as the previous prototypes. (McDonnell Douglas)

Number six (BuNo 160780) was used to test Angle of Attack and envelope extremes, one of which was tolerance to icing conditions. A KC-135 was used to spray water into the flight path of the Hornet while flying well above the freezing level. (McDonnell Douglas)

The number six prototype takes on fuel from the NATC KA-3B Skywarrior. The refueling probe is hydraulically operated with an emergency extension back up system which uses APU accumulator pressure to extend the probe. (McDonnell Douglas)

The number six prototype was painted Orange and White for high visibility. Number Six also carried a spin chute for its role as the spin test aircraft. In high angle of attack testing, it demonstrated AOA of minus 8 degrees, and plus 82 degrees. (McDonnell Douglas)

# INTO SERVICE

VFA-125, the west coast Hornet Replacement Air Group (RAG), received its first F/A-18 in February of 1981. That airplane and the two that followed it were pilot production aircraft with the first full scale production airplane being delivered in September of 1981. VFA-125 was charged with training the first Hornet instructor pilots, and as such, developed the Hornet training syllabus.

Their experiences with the F/A-18 confirmed what test pilots and the maintenance people at PAX River already knew. The F/A-18 was a remarkable performer and easy to maintain in the bargain. CAPT James Partington, Commanding Officer of VFA-125 ,was quoted as saying; *"It's amazing how steep the learning curve is in this aircraft. The aircraft teaches you how to fly it — it won't let you make a mistake."* Other instructor pilots were amazed at the ease with which the systems allowed you to become mission-proficient. A former F-4 instructor compared the months and months of F-4 training needed to achieve a consistent bombing score of 120 foot circular error of probability (CEP), with the Hornet by estimating that you could train a pilot to be a good attack pilot in the F/A-18 in about ten missions. A former A-7 pilot said that he felt more comfortable in the F-18 after 200 hours than he did in the A-7 after 2,000 hours.

VFA-125 operated a number of A-7s as target tow and air-to-air targets during the initial transition, so it was natural to compare the two airplanes. Maintenance personnel quickly discovered how easy the Hornet was to maintain, and how little maintenance it needed. The maintenance man hours per flight hour (MMH/FH) ratio averaged eighteen per month, and went as low as seven in one month. While the range of the F/A-18 was slightly less than that of the A-7, the F-18 was able to do so much more when it got to the target, on less fuel, that the question of range, which had been so worrisome to the first Navy test pilots, was put to rest. When it came to fuel endurance in air-to-air training, the F-18 was able to outstay both the A-4 and F-14 adversaries it faced.

The inauguration of the Reagan Administration resulted in a much needed defense strengthening for the United States. While many defense contracts were assured of survival in this reaffirmation of the need for a strong defense, it did not necessarily translate to profligate spending. A case in point was the F/A-18 program. John Lehman, the new Secretary of the Navy (SECNAV), negotiated a firm fixed-price contract for the 1982 production run of sixty-three Hornets which forced McDonnell Douglas and major subcontractors Northrop and Hughes to roll back prices. The new contract resulted in a 5.7% (or $1.2 million per airplane) savings for the taxpayers.

Even so, the Hornet had its critics. Rep. Joseph Addabbo (D-NY), chairman of the House Appropriations Defense Subcommittee cited a Navy operational evaluation report which noted that the F/A-18 had failed to meet three required criteria during the test program. They were; fighter escort radius of 400 nautical miles (the Hornet did 380), minimum approach speed of 132 knots at optimum angle of attack (the Hornet did 134), and maximum gross weight in the fighter escort configuration of 36,000 pounds. (the Hornet weighed in at 36,710 pounds). This all seemed like hair-splitting to Secretary Lehman (since the F/A-18 had met seventeen of twenty design goals) and he wrote to the subcommittee; *"I strongly urge your subcommittee support the full request for F/A-18 funding for Fiscal 1984."* The range problem was one which had worried the Navy from the beginning and it continued to worry them, though less and less as operational experience with the Hornet began to mitigate their concerns. (The stores carried by the Hornet could make as much as 200 to 600 nautical miles difference in the unrefueled range of the F/A-18.)

VFA-125 had discovered that refueling requirements for a strike group made up of all F/A-18s, some configured for strike, others for fighter escort, were less than those for a group of A-7s and F-14s. They also claimed that the F-18 was a superior air-to-air fighter and proved it by maneuvering for a rear hemisphere gun or AIM-9 shot on an F-14 in twenty of thirty-four engagements. The F-14 was never able to achieve a firing position on the Hornet. The impressions of VFA-125 were markedly different than those of the Navy's two Operational Evaluation Squadrons, VX-4 and VX-5, which were the operational test units which had generated the unfavorable report cited by the Hornet's critics.

An F/A-18 of VX-5 launches from the port catapult with the rudders toed-in. Project pilots of VX-5 were responsible for two weapons programs each during the tests conducted for the Operational Test and Evaluation (OPEVAL) program. (McDonnell Douglas)

VX-4 had, in fact, recommended against using the Hornet in the attack role, citing poor performance in comparison to the A-7. Opponents of this report noted that VX-4 had compared the two airplanes using A-7 flight profiles. When the F/A-18 was flown properly, it was an unquestionably better bomber or fighter than anything the Navy had. And, they said, it would also reduce manning requirements, since it was replacing two airplanes (F-4 and A-7), one of which had a two man crew. Its relatively low maintenance man hours per flight hour ratio would also help to reduce the number of mechanics needed to keep the F/A-18 in the air. In defense of the Operational Evaluation Squadrons, it should be noted that their testing procedures are designed to seek out and identify any weak points in the aircraft systems they are testing. Until the perfect airplane is invented, they are likely to continue to find faults and will keep asking the manufacturer to invent that perfect airplane.

The first Marine Corps Squadron to transition to the F/A-18 was VMFA-314, which began transition from the F-4J Phantom to the Hornet in January of 1983. LTCOL Peter Field, who was one of the Hornet test pilots, commanded VMFA-314 during the transition. They quickly discovered some pleasant differences between their new airplane and their old airplanes. The Hornet was able to exceed 1,000 nautical miles range when clean...something the Phantom could not do...and maintenance man hours per flight hour were 15-16 compared to 45-50 for the Phantom. VMFA-323 began receiving its Hornets shortly after VMFA-314, and both squadrons were completely equipped by the summer of 1983. VMFA-531 began transition shortly after, bringing to three the number of F/A-18 squadrons at Marine Corps Air Station (MCAS) El Toro, California.

The first fleet squadron to receive the F/A-18 was VFA-113 (formerly VA-113), which was the first A-7 squadron to trade-in its A-7 Corsair IIs for Hornets. VA-25 became VFA-25 when it turned in its A-7s for Hornets. These squadrons were the first to take the F/A-18 to sea on a regular cruise, when Carrier Air Wing Fourteen (CVW-14) deployed aboard USS CONSTELLATION (CV-64) in February of 1985.

**VX-4 and VX-5 pilots spent two weeks aboard USS CONSTELLATION during July of 1984, testing the Hornet and its weapons systems before the F/A-18 made its first operational deployment. (McDonnell Douglas)**

(Above) A pair of F/A-18s of VX-4 during the operational test program. VX-4 created consternation among Naval Air Warfare planners in 1982 when they recommended against using the Hornet in the attack role. (Norm Taylor)

(Above) The Navy planned to replace the fleet's light attacker, the A-7, with the F/A-18, and the criticism of the F/A-18's range, endurance, landing weight, and the ejection seat by VX-4 were unsettling. The mission profiles flown were not written for the F/A-18 and the landing weight concerns centered around returning with ordnance and having insufficient fuel for several landing passes.

The east coast RAG was established with the re-activation of an attack squadron which had been de-commissioned in 1969. VFA-106 was resurrected at NAS Cecil Field, Florida on 27 April 1984. Two other new F/A-18 squadrons were activated in 1983 when VFA-131 and VFA-132 were commissioned as members of CVW-13 at NAS Lemoore. The squadrons were then transferred to NAS Cecil to become the east coast's first operational Hornet squadrons. They went to sea aboard USS CORAL SEA (CV-43) in October of 1985 for a Mediterranean cruise with the Sixth Fleet. The CORAL SEA cruise provided the first operational test of the versatility of the F/A-18. Four Hornet squadrons were aboard, VFA-131, VFA-132, VMFA-314, and VMFA-323.

The Naval Reserve received its first Hornet Squadron in January of 1984 with the redesignation of VA-303 to VFA-303, based at NAS Lemoore. As the production lines heated up, more new Hornet squadrons were commissioned, working toward the eventual goal of forty-two F/A-18 squadrons. New Marine Corps Squadrons included VMFA-115, VMFA-122, VMFA-451 and VMFA-251. New Navy squadrons were VFA-136, VFA-137, VFA-192, VFA-195, VFA-151, VFA-15 and VFA-161. Scheduled for conversion to the Hornet are VA-146 and VA-147, which will become VFA squadrons when transition is completed.

(Left) A flight of Hornets of VX-4, the *Evaluators*, over the Pacific near their home base at Point Mugu, California. VX-4 conducted carrier trials and weapons tests with the F/A-18. (McDonnell Douglas via Norm Taylor)

(Left) An F/A-18A of VFA-125 the first Hornet operational training squadron. VFA-125 began training operations at NAS Lemoore in late 1980. (McDonnell Douglas via Norm Taylor)

VFA-125, (formerly VA-125) was the West Coast A-7 RAG before changing to the Hornet. The squadron's first Hornet is chased by one of its A-7E Corsair IIs early in 1981. (McDonnell Douglas)

An F/A-18B two-seat Hornet demonstrates it's 'over the top' vertical performance on a factory acceptance flight high over a wintry Mississippi River not far from the McDonnell Aircraft Company in St. Louis. (McDonnell Douglas)

A mixed formation of F/A-18As and Bs of VFA-125. Hornet pilots were, for the most part, former A-7 pilots with limited air-to-air experience. They became instant fighter pilots when they transferred to the F/A-18 and quickly proved that they could be successful fighter pilots because of the F/A-18's outstanding maneuverability. (McDonnell Douglas via Norm Taylor)

(Above) An F/A-18B Hornet on an operational acceptance flight by McDonnell Douglas test pilots over the muddy Mississippi river during May of 1983. (McDonnell Douglas)

(Above) An F/A-18B two seater armed with a pair of AIM-7 Sparrow missiles on the fuselage and an AIM-9 Sidewinder on each wingtip conducts a test flight during 1982. Sunlight is shining through the slots in the leading edge extensions revealing their position. (McDonnell Douglas)

(Below) This trio of current production aircraft from the McDonnell Douglas factory at Lambert Field, St. Louis including an F-15 Eagle, F/A-18 Hornet, and AV-8B Harrier II, says more about the status of McDonnell Douglas as a prime defense contractor than thousands of words. (McDonnell Douglas)

(Above) Head on the slim YF-17 reveals its simple light land based type landing gear, strakes on the sides of the nose, slots in the leading edge extensions, and lack of underwing pylons. (Northrop)

(Below) The F/A-18's heavy beefed-up carrier landing gear is one of the principal differences between the Hornet and the earlier YF-17 lightweight fighter. The internal boarding ladder folds into the bottom of the port leading edge extension. (McDonnell Douglas)

(Below) An F/A-18A Hornet loaded with AIM-9 Sidewinders on the wingtips, MK-83 practice bombs on the outboard pylons, fuel tanks on inboard and centerline pylons, Ford Aerospace ASS-38 forward-looking infra-red (FLIR) pod on left fuselage, and Martin Marietta Laser Spot Tracker/Strike Camera (LST/SCAM) on the right fuselage station. (McDonnell Douglas)

An F/-18A Hornet chained down aboard ship with the wings in the folded position. The small port in the center of the nose behind the radome is the gun port for the M-61 Vulcan 20mm six barrel rotary cannon. (McDonnell Douglas)

A Hornet of VMFA-314 test fires a Sidewinder from the wingtip pylon. The AIM-9 Sidewinder was developed by the Naval Ordnance Test Station, China Lake, California in the 1940s. The latest Navy versions are the AIM-9L and M with all-aspect acquisition and intercept capabilities against high speed, maneuvering targets. (McDonnell Douglas)

An F/A-18A testing what may become the optimum air-to-air configuration — a pair of Sidewinders on each outboard pylon. These are Blue painted inert missiles, suggesting that this flight was for aerodynamic testing of the paired missile configuration. (McDonnell Douglas)

(Above) An F/A-18 takes off with Sparrows, Sidewinders, and a pair of 500 pound Snakeye low drag bombs on the centerline. The Hornet can carry up to 17,000 pounds of ordnance on nine external stations. (McDonnell Douglas)

The first flight of the F/A-18 armed with the McDonnell Douglas AGM-84 Harpoon antiship missiles was made from NAS China Lake in August of 1985. (McDonnell Douglas)

(Below) VMFA-314 Hornet firing an AIM-9L from the left wingtip station. The AIM-9L weighs 188 pounds at launch, has a motor burn time of sixty seconds, and a range of 11 miles. It is manufactured by the Ford Aerospace & Communications Corporation, Aeronautical Division. (McDonnell Douglas)

The Hughes AN/APG-65 radar provides terrain avoidance, precision velocity updates, sea search, ground moving target track, fixed target track, and air-to-surface ranging in the ground mode. In the air-to-air mode, it provides velocity search, range-while-search, track-while-scan, raid assessment, gun director mode, and three missile attack modes (boresight, vertical acquisition, head-up display). The built in test (BIT) system and plug-in modules make it easy to maintain. (McDonnell Douglas)

Nose gear doors of an F/A-18. The vents on the fuselage sides are gun bay gas vents which prevent a build up of dangerous gases when the gun is fired. (Dave Mason)

The nose gear of an F/A-18 with the catapult shuttle link in the retracted position. When the aircraft is positioned over the catapult shuttle, the link automatically lowers to engage the shuttle for launch. (Dave Mason)

Technicians check the nose gear of an F/A-18 at the McDonnell Douglas plant. The bar (right) extending from the landing gear strut is the catapult shuttle link bar. (McDonnell Douglas)

The nose gear bay of an F/A-18. The light on the center of the gear strut is the landing light, while the three colored lights below it are used with the carrier's mirror landing system. (McDonnell Douglas and Dave Mason)

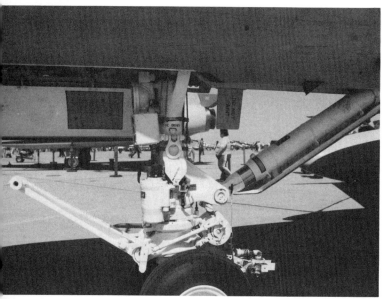

The port main gear well of an F/A-18. The multi-ported panel in front of the gear well is one of the chaff/flair dispensers. A second dispenser is located on the starboard side. (Dave Mason)

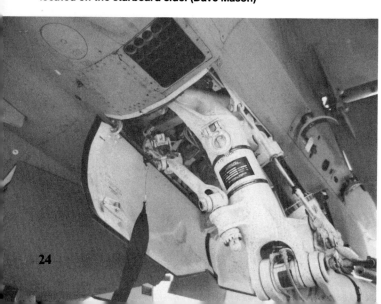

The first TF-18A (later F/A-18B) BuNo 160781 armed with AIM-9L Sidewinders on the wingtips and AIM-7F Sparrows on the fuselage during a test hop over the Pacific. (McDonnell Douglas via Norm Taylor)

The SJU-5/A ejection seat used in both the F/A-18A and F/A-18B.

The heart of the Hornet weapons system, the APG-65 radar.

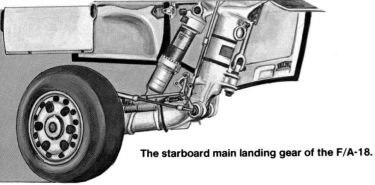

The starboard main landing gear of the F/A-18.

The Hornet's tail hook is neatly tucked in between the engine nozzles at the rear of the fuselage. (Dave Mason)

One of eight formation strip lights on the Hornet. The brightness of these lights is controlled by a vernier switch in the cockpit. The Marine Corps logo is Dark Gray against the Light Gray background. (Dave Mason)

Tailhook extension is free-fall, assisted by a nitrogen charge. The hook is held down to ensure arresting cable engagement by a damper in the retraction actuator cylinder. (Dave Mason)

Lateral motion of the tail hook is dampened by a liquid spring in the hook shank. This helps prevent 'hook skip' when landing on a pitching deck.

(Above) A McDonnell Douglas Aircraft Company electronics technician installs the AIMES computer in a Hornet on the St. Louis factory ramp. Ease of access is one of the keys to the maintainability of the Hornet, which gives the F/A-18 the best maintenance man hour/flight hour ratio of any modern fighter. (McDonnell Douglas)

(Below) The Avionic Fault Tree Analyzer (AFTA) helps maintenance personnel detect and fix electronic failures through a computer diagnostic program. (McDonnell Douglas)

The heads-up-display (HUD) and gunsight glass panels are mounted on the top of the instrument panel anti-glare shield. (Dave Mason)

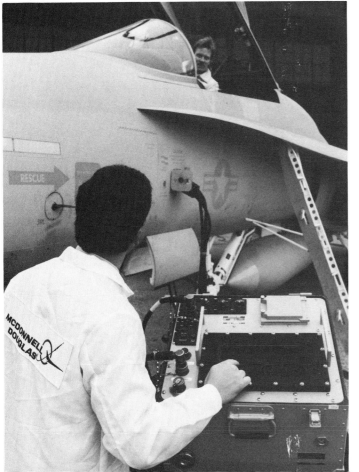

The canopy opening actuator rod is located behind the pilot's ejection seat. The 'V' shaped assembly on the canopy rail is the canopy locking lug. (Dave Mason)

The F/A-18A number three prototype arrives overhead USS AMERICA to begin carrier suitability tests.

The number five F/A-18 prototype in formation with another McDonnell Douglas aircraft the F-15 Eagle during factory test flights prior to delivery to the Navy at Pax River.

The bright Orange and White paint scheme made the number six prototype easier to track during spin tests. Number six was the only prototype to carry this scheme. (McDonnell Douglas)

Blue Angels One is flown by the team leader, Commander Gil Rud. The Blue Angels are an important recruiting asset for the Navy, inspiring many young men to seek a career in Naval Aviation. (McDonnell Douglas)

Libyan Air Force MiG-25 Foxbat A all weather fighters shadowed Sixth Fleet operations in the Gulf of Sidra during March of 1986. The Foxbats made no attempt to engage the Hornets even though they were fully armed with AA-6 and AA-8 missiles. (via Mule Holmberg)

An F/A-18A of VFA-106 flown by LT John 'O.D.' O'Donnell pulls over the top in a loop. (Author)

An F/A-18A Hornet of Marine Fighter Attack Squadron 531 (VMFA-531). This Hornet is assigned to the squadron commander, COL Jim Lucas.

An F/A-18A of VMFA-323 escorts a Soviet IL 38 May anti-submarine aircraft as it flies a reconnaissance mission against the CORAL SEA Battle Group during April of 1986.

(Below) The retraction sequence of the Hornet's main landing gear is demonstrated by an F/A-18A of Marine Fighter Attack Squadron 323 (VMFA-323). (USMC)

(Above) An F/A-18A Hornet of the U.S. Navy Strike Warfare Center during a visit to Luke AFB, Arizona on 23 February 1986. The lightning bolt and 'Strike' are in Dark Gray. (Brian Rogers via Norm Taylor)

## F/A-18B

LOT 4
**BLOCK 5 (4)**
161354 thru 161357

**BLOCK 6 (1)**
161360

LOT 5
**BLOCK 8 (4)**
161704, 161707, 161711 161714

**BLOCK 9 (4)**
161719, 161723, 161727 161733

**BLOCK 10 (3)**
161740, 161746, 161924

LOT 6
**BLOCK 11 (3)**
161932, 161938, 161943

**BLOCK 12 (1)**
161947

LOT 7
**BLOCK 14 (3)**
162402, 162408, 162413

**BLOCK 15 (2)**
162419, 162427

LOT 8
**BLOCK 17 (3)**
162836, 162842, 162850

**BLOCK 18 (4)**
162857, 162864, 162870, 162876

**BLOCK 19 (1)**
162885

LOT 9
**BLOCK 20 (3)**
163104, 163110, 163115

**BLOCK 21 (1)**
163123

**BLOCK 22 (0)**

## F/A-18 A

LOT 4
**BLOCK 5 (3)**
161353, 161358, 161359

**BLOCK 6 (8)**
161361 thru 161367, 161519

**BLOCK 7 (9)**
161520 thru 161528

LOT 5
**BLOCK 8 (10)**
161702, 161703, 161705, 161706, 161708, 161709, 161710, 161712, 161713, 161715

**BLOCK 9 (17)**
161716 thru 161718, 161720 thru 161722, 161724 thru 161726, 161728 thru 161732, 161734 thru 161736

**BLOCK 10 (23)**
161737 thru 161739 161741 thru 161745 161747 thru 161761

LOT 6
**BLOCK 11 (17)**
161925 thru 161931 161933 thru 161937 161939 thru 161942 161944

**BLOCK 12 (20)**
161945, 161946, 161948 thru 161965

**BLOCK 13 (22)**
161966 thru 161987

LOT 7
**BLOCK 14 (18)**
162934 thru 162401 162403 thru 162407 162409 thru 162412, 162414

**BLOCK 15 (28)**
162415 thru 162418, 162420 thru 162426, 162428 thru 162444

**BLOCK 16 (33)**
162445 thru 162477

LOT 8
**BLOCK 17 (24)**
162826 thru 162835, 162837 thru 162841, 162843 thru 162849, 162851, 162852

**BLOCK 18 (25)**
162853 thru 162856 162858 thru 162863 162865 thru 162869 162871 thru 162875 162877 thru 162881

**BLOCK 19 (27)**
162882 thru 162884 162886 thru 162909

LOT 9
**BLOCK 20 (24)**
163092 thru 163103 163105 thru 163109 163111 thru 163114 163116 thru 163118

**BLOCK 21 (26)**
163119 thru 163122 163124 thru 163145

**BLOCK 22 (30)**
163146 thru 163175

30

# F/A-18 ORIENTATION RIDE
## DAY ONE

My camera bag was shot to the rear of the right console by the force of the acceleration from the twin GE F-404 engines of our F/A-18B. You expect dramatics in the performance department when you climb into a jet fighter, but I couldn't remember being this impressed by initial acceleration, even in the F-15. I was really looking forward to the rest of this flight, and had been since it was first proposed by Roy Stafford.

Roy is a former Marine Phantom pilot who has maintained his service friendships. He is also a T-34 owner and a close friend who has gone out of his way to encourage and assist me wherever possible. It was his relationship with Colonel Jim Lucas, Commander of the Marine Aviation Training Support Group at NAS Cecil Field, that had gotten me into the backseat of the Navy's newest fighter. There is more to being a fighter pilot than just yanking and banking, and a major portion of the fighter pilot's time is spent in getting ready to fly, so the Navy was not about to let me just waltz onto the base and go fly. Before I could fly I had to go through the military aviators quadrennial...the dreaded ritual...the physiological lecture series and trip to altitude in the altitude chamber. This was to be followed by a survival techniques lecture, ejection seat orientation, and a dynamic seat shot. They also wanted to put me through the water survival training, which included swimming a mile in a flight suit, but agreed to waive that requirement since we were not going to be over water for this flight.

If you are ever tempted to get a little blasé about flying in a jet fighter, just reading the military orders that authorize such adventures for a civilian will throw you off stride. My orders came from CINCLANTFLT NORFOLK VA (Commander in Chief Atlantic Fleet) and were addressed to STRKFITRON ONE ZERO SIX (Strike Fighter Squadron 106), with information copies to CNO (Chief of Naval Operations) WASHINGTON DC, COMNAVAIRLANT (Commander Naval Air Forces Atlantic) NORFOLK, COMSTRIKFIGHTWINGSLANT (Commander Strike Fighter Wings Atlantic) CECIL FIELD, CHINFO (Chief of Information) WASHINGTON, and COMLATWING ONE (Commander Light Attack Wing 1) CECIL FIELD. The text of the orders was no less arcane than all of the acronyms used for the addressees.
SUBJ: CIV FLT AUTH
A. STRKFITRON ONE ZERO SIX 301303Z MAR 87
B. OPNAVINST 3710.7L 1. ORIG TAKES REF A FORAC.

**An F/A-18B of VFA-106 'Gladiators' chocked on the ramp at Carswell AFB, Fort Worth, Texas on 8 December 1985. The side number '357' is in Black on the nose and tip of the vertical tail. (Brian Rogers via Norm Taylor)**

2. REF A RQSTD AUTH FOR ORIENTATION/INDOC FLTS FOR MR. LOU DRENDEL IN VFA-106 F/A-18B AIRCRAFT FM
CECIL FIELD FL.

3. CONTINGENT UPON SUCCESSFUL COMPLETION OF REF B NAPTP/NAWSTP REQMTS,
PERGRA FOR ONE TIME ORIENTATION/INDOC FLT WITHIN PROVISIONS OF REF B
PARA 210. FLT TO BE CONDUCTED ON NIB. NAWSTP REQMTS WAIVED IF FLT
CONDUCTED ENTIRELY OVER LAND. BT

Naval Air Station Cecil Field is just west of Jacksonville, Florida. The signs at the entrance proclaim it a "Master Jet Base", and the almost constant activity in the traffic pattern is ample evidence of that status. If, as the popular poster proclaims; "Jet Noise is The Sound of Freedom!", then there is a whole lot of freedom in northern Florida. The East Coast Replacement Air Group (RAG) trains F/A-18 Hornet, A-7E Corsiar II, and A-4 Skyhawk pilots at Cecil and the number of aircraft movements rivals some of the busier commercial airports. But my ride in the F/A-18 still seemed a long way off on that monday morning as I headed for building 198 and my encounter with the chamber. I had been through an altitude chamber three times before, but my most recent experiences were with the Air Force, and I was curious about how Navy procedures would differ. Captain Marty Wilcox, USMC, my escort from VFA-106 was there to see that I got checked in and started on the Physiology lectures.

LT Russell Lawry started us right off with the symptoms and dangers of hypoxia...oxygen starvation. The principle danger to a pilot is, of course, mental confusion and ultimately, unconsciousness which is likely to lead to a smoking hole in the ground. The symptoms range from belligerence to euphoria, with side effects that include numbness or a tingling sensation. The magic line which has been drawn in the atmosphere by most authorities is 10,000 feet. Above that altitude the average body cannot maintain the blood/oxygen saturation needed for normal functioning, and supplemental oxygen is needed. Between 30,000 and 34,000 feet, positive pressure breathing is required to get the oxygen into the blood stream. And speaking of blood, the Navy says that giving a pint of blood requires grounding for four days...if you are flying from a land base. On the other hand, if you are operating from a carrier, they ground you for 30 days after blood donation! That is the accepted difference in stress levels between the two environments.

Since oxygen starvation, and the resulting hypoxic effects are seldom instantaneous, the whole point of demonstrating them is to enable the aviator to recognize the symptoms when he has them.

*AK 100*, an F/A-18A of VFA-131 was assigned to the Air Group Commander aboard USS CORAL SEA during OPERATION PRAIRIE FIRE, the Gulf of Sidra freedom of navigation operations during February and March of 1986.

The Hornet is an international fighter flown by (right to left, top to bottom) U.S. Navy, Canadian Armed Forces, Spanish Air Force, and Royal Australian Air Force.

The Hornet's heavy duty landing gear has ample travel to cushion the impact of a carrier landing or a hard landing on a short field ashore.

LT John O'Donnell in *AD 312* demonstrates the low speed maneuverability of the Hornet by flying formation with Roy Stafford in his T-34B Mentor over central Florida during April of 1987.

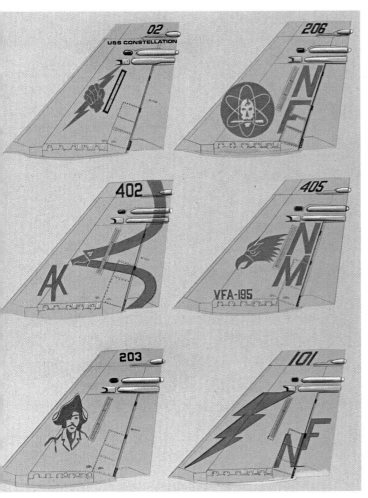

Hornet tail markings; (clockwise from upper left) VFA-25, VFA-151, VFA-195, VFA-161, VFA-132, and VFA-137.

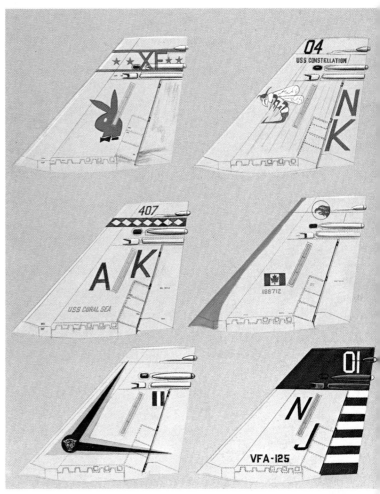

Hornet tail markings; (clockwise from upper left) VX-4, VFA-113, 409 Squadron Canadian Armed Forces, VFA-125, 2 Operational Conversion Unit, Royal Australian Air Force, and VMFA-323.

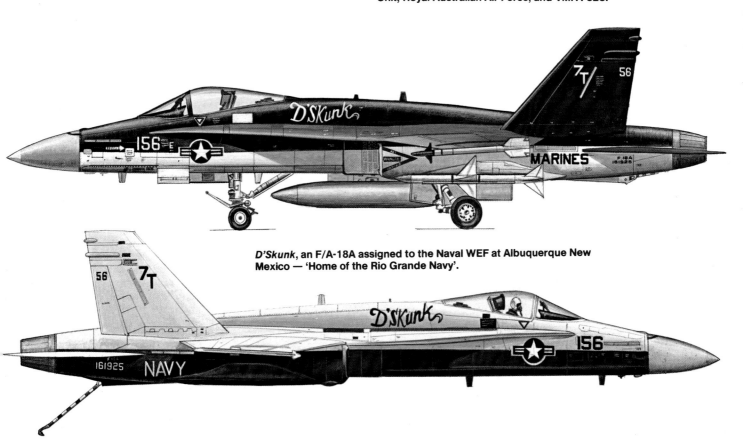

*D'Skunk*, an F/A-18A assigned to the Naval WEF at Albuquerque New Mexico — 'Home of the Rio Grande Navy'.

# F/A-18A/B Ejection Seat

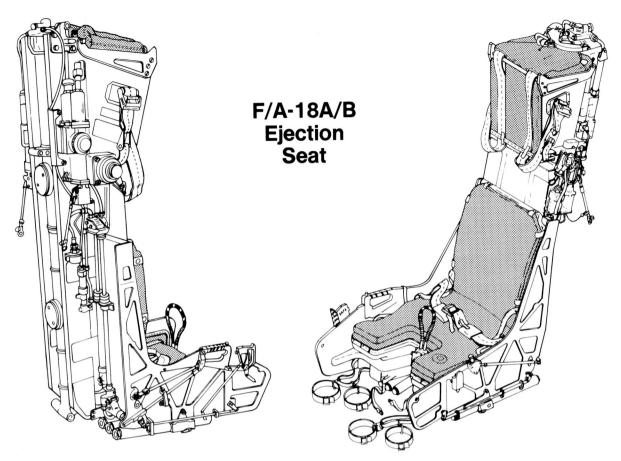

The higher the altitude, the less time he will have to recognize the onset of hypoxia. At 18,000 feet, it may take 30 minutes before anything happens. But at 25,000 feet, you only have 4 minutes to do something about the lack of oxygen! The geometric degression of reaction time continues as you ascend; unless you smoke, or work in a smoke-filled environment. In that case, you are already at nine to ten thousand feet before you step into the cockpit and you are that far behind the non-smoking aviator. That, along with the warning that excess caffeine or sugar will actually reduce your stamina and ability to withstand hypoxia, sort of kills the menu for the fighter pilot's traditional breakfast, which is; "A smoke, a coke, and a puke."

Another universally accepted rule is; "12 hours from bottle to throttle". That is a generous interpretation, since studies have shown that subjects with .08% blood/alcohol levels (less than what is required to be "legally" drunk) are making mistakes at the alarming frequency of 61% of the time fourteen hours after their last drink!

For pilots flying fighter or attack aircraft, the most commonly encountered form of hypoxia is G-induced hypoxia. As the fangs come out and the G comes on, blood is drained from the upper extremities and pools in the lower extremities. Since most of us think with our uppermost extremity, (there are exceptions) loss of blood/oxygen means impairment of the thought process. The fighter pilot's protection against G is his anti-G suit. LT Lawry warned us that the G suit might provide up to 1.5 Gs of extra tolerance...if it was properly fitted. His definition of a proper fit was; "If it's comfortable, it probably doesn't fit correctly." Since the F/A-18 can generate an onset G-rate of up to 16 Gs and, even with the limiter in operation can sustain up to 10 Gs, the importance of developing G tolerance is evident. The pilot's second line of defense is the Anti-G maneuver, or L1M1, or grunting maneuver. This is an isometric contraction in which you tense your legs, stomach and chest muscles by grunting against the pull of G. If this exercise is performed correctly, it can increase your G tolerance by up to 2 Gs. However, if it is done incorrectly, it can actually impair your tolerance. The recommended procedure is a forced three second exhale, followed by a one second inhale, then a repeat of this, followed by a hard grunt against the G.

Altitude is also likely to cause you trouble if you have any suggestion of a block in your eustaceon tubes. These are the passages that allow gas to pass from your inner to outer ears. Ear blocks are characterized by muffled sound and, depending upon their severity, pain. In the case of a severe block, a perforated ear drum may result. Eustaceon tube blocks most commonly occur when an individual has a cold, or when operating in an extremely dry atmosphere. It pays to keep clearing your ears as you descend, and this can be done by chewing, yawning, or performing the valsalvo maneuver, which consists of holding your nose, and blowing against it. Sinus blocks, if rare, are much more serious. They can cause debilitating pain, and the only relief from them is ascent to higher altitude. There have been documented cases of pilots losing control of their aircraft because of the pain of a sinus block. That pain was described by Lawry as; "having someone stick an icepick into your head and twirling it around." A badly blown sinus can permanently ground an aviator. Other pressure problems can be caused by eating foods that generate a lot of gas prior to a flight. This can cause severe cramping if that gas gets trapped in the intestines. But that problem can be relieved in traditional, if smelly, ways.

There was a litany of other physiological traps awaiting the aviator, including nitrogen in the blood, which can lead to the bends. Fatigue, stress, hyper- and hypo-glycemia, and drugs are also high on the list of hazards to pilots. One of the primary rules in military flying is that you never self-medicate, and that includes over-the-counter drugs, even something as bland as aspirin. (The most dramatic example of the negative results of self medication was the crash of the EA-6B Prowler aboard ship a few years ago, which killed several sailors and did millions of dollars of damage. The pilot was flying with a bad head cold and had been medicating himself with anti-histamines. He was not quite up to a night carrier landing.)

Hospitalman Paul Bedsole opened his presentation on the effects of sensory disorientation with a demonstration in the revolving chair. A volunteer was asked to sit in the chair, close his eyes, and put his head down. Bedsole got the chair turning with several good swings, then let it wind down until it stopped. The volunteer was

An F/A-18B of VFA-106 on the transit line at McChord AFB, Washington on 19 January 1986. VA-106 was equipped with A-4 Skyhawks when decommissioned in November of 1969, but sprang to life again in 1984 as VFA-106, the East Coast Fleet Replacement Squadron for the F/A-18 Hornet. (D. Remington via Norm Taylor)

asked to move his head left, right, then center it again. Then he was asked which direction the chair was moving. He indicated that it had stopped and then started in the opposite direction, when in fact it had not been moved again after it started.

This disorientation was caused by the movement of the fluid in his inner-ear canals. There are three canals, and each is filled with a viscous fluid. Tiny hairs in the canals sense the motion of this fluid and send signals to the brain to indicate pitch, roll, yaw, and acceleration or deceleration. In VFR (Visual Flight Rules) conditions, the visual inputs overcome the erroneous information transmitted by the inner ear. The visual inputs presented by aircraft instruments are not strong enough to overcome the visceral inputs without a strong mental commitment to the accuracy of their information. Even experienced instrument pilots report debilitating attacks of vertigo when abrupt head movements are made during instrument flight. A universal vertigo-producer is close formation flying in clouds.

I can attest to that, having experienced it several times myself. My experiences had been limited to climbing or descending through a few thousand feet of clouds, and didn't last for more than a few minutes. But in those few minutes I would have sworn that we were in a turn and it was all I could do to refrain from making unnecessary control movements. A more prolonged exposure would no doubt have the sweat glands working overtime. Roaring cases of vertigo are usually recognizable, and if the pilot has the will to overcome them, he can survive. But there is an even more dangerous type of vertigo. When flying at night, or over the ocean on a cloudy day with poor visibility and lack of well-defined horizon, it is possible for the pilot to enter a spin or "graveyard spiral". At first the canals sense the motion and relay the signal to the brain, but if the spin or spiral remains constant, those tiny hairs in fluid in the ear canal will return to their "straight and level" position, sending a reassuring, but deadly erroneous signal.

The most dangerous form of vertigo is Coriolis, which results from a combination of conflicting signals being sent from the inner ear canals to the brain. This is caused by abrupt head movements in several different directions while flying on instruments. It can cause visual disorientation, as evidenced by rapid flickering of the eyes. Coriolis was demonstrated by another chair volunteer.

Bedsole emphasized this old, but effective, demonstration of the effects of vertigo by reading a report on the loss of an A-6 Intruder. During a night approach to the USS KENNEDY, the pilot had unhooked his oxygen mask from the right side of his helmet. He was required to make several radio transmissions while flying in IMC (Instrument Meteorological Conditions). Each time he transmitted, he turned his head to the left to speak into the microphone in the oxygen mask, which was hanging from the left side of his helmet. The result of those several head turns was a severe case of vertigo, which resulted in loss of control of the aircraft...and a crash.

Bedsole continued his presentation with a review of the limitations and idiosyncrasies of the human eye, explaining the difference in the eye's photoreceptor cells (rods and cones). Cones pick up fine detail and color, and are primary receptors for day vision. Rods provide night vision. The value of scanning, either the instrument panel two feet in front of you, or the sky miles in front of you, is demonstrated by the physiological blind spots that result from the location of the rods and cones. Both serve you well, but only if you move your eyes to allow them to focus. The night vision blind spot, without scanning, is one inch at three feet. But that equates to 106 feet at 3,000 feet, which means that you could miss seeing a bomber at little more than a half a mile at night!

After hearing about the limitations and fallibilities of the body I had become so accustomed to, I was less than eager to subject it to the altitude chamber...especially after having been advised that I would not be allowed to remove my mask and experience hypoxia, since I was over 40 and "more susceptible to dying!" (In the military, everyone is mortal, but some are more mortal than others.) We all trooped down to the supply window, drew our helmets and masks, and filed into the chamber. We were seated in the chamber and given a short orientation of the control panel for each station and when everyone was thoroughly checked out and on oxygen, we began our ascent to 25,000 feet.

In the jet age, most people who have flown commercially have routinely climbed right past 25,000 feet without a mask and without much discomfort. What many do not realize is that the airliner cabin, in addition to being filled with air, is also pressurized to an altitude of no more than 8,000 feet (this is also the case in most combat cockpits). But in a war, with assorted bits and pieces of hot lead flying through the air, that nice, environmentally consistent cocoon you are sitting in may get punctured, so the military plans for loss of pressurization, and trains for it with the altitude chamber. So, while we would have oxygen, we would not have pressurization, and as a reminder of what that meant, a rubber surgeon's glove, bound at the wrist like a balloon, was suspended from the ceiling of the chamber. We watched it expand as we climbed, all the time envisioning our intestines performing similar distentions.

Upon reaching 25,000 feet, those who were under 40, (and not in danger of imminent death) were paired off and allowed to remove their masks for a demonstration of hypoxia. They played patty cake for a few minutes until a loss of coordination and euphoria ended the demonstration. They were all urged to replace their masks as soon as they recognized the effects of hypoxia, and all were able to do so, though the mental confusion was evident in most as they fumbled for the mask attachment and the oxygen switch on their control panels. The only problem encountered in descent is keeping your ears cleared. If you allow pressure to build, it can lead to a

Canadian Armed Forces Hornet squadron insignias.

Royal Australian Air Force Hornet squadron insignias.

This TF-18A of VFA-106 is assigned to the squadron commander and has the unit insignia in full color instead of the subdued Gray's carried by the rest of the squadron.

The author at 500 knots and 300 feet during the run in to the Rodman target range. There is a canary feather smile under that mask!

F/A-18 cockpit displays and panels are exactly reproduced in the F/A-18 cockpit simulator. (McDonnell Douglas)

An F/A-18A Hornet in its natural environment, on the deck of an aircraft carrier.

# F/A-18A Instrument Panel

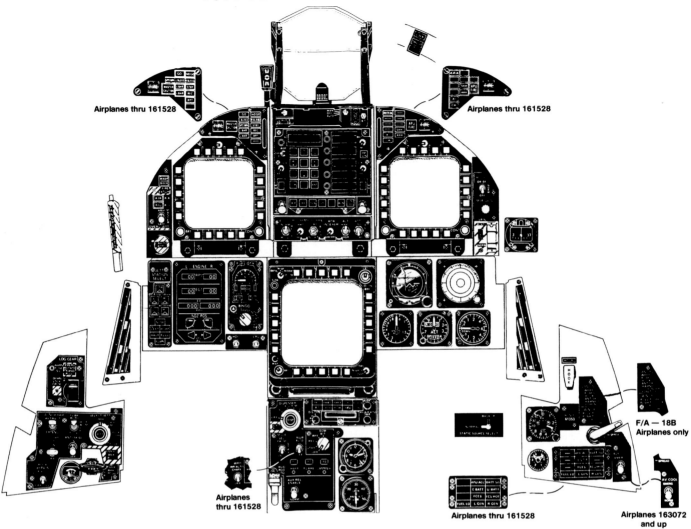

Airplanes thru 161528

Airplanes thru 161528

Airplanes thru 161528

Airplanes thru 161528

F/A — 18B Airplanes only

Airplanes 163072 and up

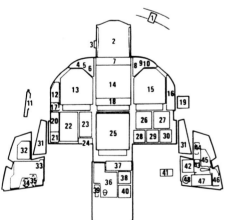

1. LOCK SHOOT LIGHTS
2. HEADS UP DISPLAY (HUD)
3. ANGLE OF ATTACK INDEXER LIGHTS
4. LEFT ENGINE FIRE WARNING/EXTINGUISHER LIGHT
5. MASTER CAUTION LIGHT
6. LEFT WARNING/CAUTION/ADVISORY LIGHTS
7. HUD VIDEO CAMERA CONTROL
8. RIGHT WARNING/CAUTION/ADVISORY LIGHTS
9. AUXILIARY POWER UNIT FIRE WARNING/EXTINGUISHER LIGHT
10. RIGHT ENGINE FIRE WARNING/EXTINGUISHER LIGHT
11. CANOPY INTERNAL JETTISON HANDLE
12. MASTER ARM PANEL
13. LEFT DIGITAL DISPLAY INDICATOR (DDI)
14. UPFRONT CONTROL PANEL
15. RIGHT DIGITAL DISPLAY INDICATOR (DDI)
16. MAP GAIN/SPIN RECOVERY PANEL
17. EMERGENCY JETTISON BUTTON
18. HUD CONTROL
19. STANDBY MAGNETIC COMPASS
20. STATION JETTISON SELECT
21. LANDING GEAR AND FLAP POSITION LIGHTS
22. ENGINE MONITOR INDICATOR (EMI)
   • L & R RPM
   • L & R EGT
   • L & R FUEL FLOW
   • L & R NOZZLE POSITION
   • L & R OIL PRESSURE
23. FUEL QUANTITY INDICATOR
24. HEADING AND COURSE SET SWITCHES
25. HORIZONTAL INDICATOR (HI)
26. STANDBY ATTITUDE REFERENCE INDICATOR
27. AZIMUTH INDICATOR;BLANK PANEL (SOME AIRPLANES)
28. STANDBY AIRSPEED INDICATOR
29. STANDBY ALTIMETER
30. STANDBY RATE OF CLIMB INDICATOR
31. ENVIRONMENT CONTROL LOUVERS
32. LANDING GEAR HANDLE AND WARNING TONE SILENCE BUTTON

33. SELECT JETTISON BUTTON
34. BRAKE ACCUMULATOR PRESSURE GAGE
35. EMERGENCY BRAKE AND PARKING BRAKE HANDLE
36. DISPENSER/ECM PANEL
37. RWR CONTROL INDICATOR;BLANK PANEL (SOME AIRPLANES)
38. CLOCK
39. RUDDER PEDAL ADJUST LEVER
40. COCKPIT ALTIMETER
41. STATIC SOURCE SELECT
42. RADAR ALTIMETER
43. AIRCRAFT BUREAU NUMBER
44. ARRESTING HOOK HANDLE AND LIGHT
45. LANDING CHECKLIST AND WING FOLD SWITCH
46. FLIGHT COMPUTER COOL SWITCH
47. CAUTION LIGHTS PANEL (GEN TIE on airplanes 162394 and up)
48. HYD 1 AND HYD 2 PRESSURE INDICATOR

**LT John 'OD' O'Donnell in 'Roman 86/2' joins up over central Florida after completing a practice bombing run on the Rodman bombing range. (Author)**

punctured ear drum, and if you don't clear periodically on the way down, that pressure can build quickly and become progressively harder to clear. As we left the chamber, I was still clearing my ears. And I would continue to do so for the next two days...another side effect of oxygen use at high altitude.

The chamber ride was followed by an hour of survival training and then the ejection seat orientation. All Naval Aviators are required to make at least one dynamic seat shot in their careers. I had never experienced this ride, (the Air Force has no such requirement) and was not particularly looking forward to it. I had been subjected to all kinds of stories about the ejection seat trainer. A neighbor, who is a USAF veteran and former T-38 instructor, assured me that the dynamic seat shot was a 40-G experience. My mind boggled at that, since I am sure I don't have a 40-G spinal column. Stafford assured me that it was no more that 3 or 4 Gs, but I still wasn't looking forward to it. I was not reassured to learn that the real seat has an initial acceleration of up to 250 Gs! (This is caused by the catapult system which initiates seat separation from the aircraft, and lasts a fraction of a second. When the rocket engine fires, the acceleration is much smoother and is reported to be in the 8-12 G range.)

Two pilots who had been forced to eject from an F/A-18B the previous week reported that the opening shock of the parachute was more violent than the ejection. I was not reassured by that news either, and was even less enthusiastic about a possible ejection when I found out that the parachute which will save your life is probably going to break your bones when you land. The main canopy is a mere seventeen feet in diameter, and descent rates of up to 45 feet per second are routine! In contrast, the thirty foot elliptical canopy I used in the 82nd Airborne had a descent rate of 18 feet per second, and the twenty-eight foot flat canopies used in most other military parachutes let you down at 25 feet per second. The thinking behind the seventeen foot canopy is that most ejections are going to be over water, and hitting the water at that speed will not cause a problem. That's O.K. for the Navy...but what about the Marines? Are they really that tough? Evidently not, since Martin Baker, the manufacturer of the seat, is working on a modification which will not be as simple as it seems. The parachute is packed behind the headrest, and the pilots don't want any width increase in the headrest because that creates a visibility restriction during air combat maneuvering.

By 1400 (2 PM to you civilians) all but one of my classmates had

completed their training, been given their papers, and were on their way home. Two of us had to sustain the dynamic seat shot, and we were fitted with torso harnesses for the exercise. The torso harness is a combination parachute harness/vest which contains the attachment fittings for your lap belt and parachute risers, also doubling as a shoulder harness. Getting into the torso harness is something like putting on a girdle (I guess), and (I guess) is just about as comfortable. Lawry's rule applied to the torso harness as well...if it's comfortable, it's not right. Mine was obviously right. Once fitted, I waddled out to the trainer, which is located in a separate building. "Building" may not be the right word. "Room" would be more like it, since this building is no more than twenty feet square, though it does have a thirty foot ceiling! The seat is situated in the middle of this room, in the middle of a platform five steps above the floor. The platform is surrounded by the mechanism which propels the seat up the rails that reach to the ceiling. As I mounted those steps, the thought crossed my mind that gallows and guillotines were also mounted on platforms.

Once strapped into the seat, I was instructed to assume the correct position, which is; head firmly against the headrest, with chin elevated ten degrees, (are they checking that with a transit?) shoulders and back firmly against the seat back, elbows and arms firmly against sides, buttocks firmly against seat back, thighs flat against the seat, with the outside of the thighs against the side of the seat, and the heels flat on the deck with the feet on the rudder pedals. I can tell you, this makes a great isometric exercise! You could lose a few pounds if you had your own ejection seat to practice on, and I sure felt like I was sweating off a few right then! The training officer told me that I would initiate the ejection by pulling the handle between my legs, on his command. He barked; "EJECT! EJECT! EJECT!" I yanked...BANG!...aaargh, where's the nearest chiropracter? The shot was probably no more than three or four Gs, but it was instantaneous, and I must not have had my eyeballs caged, because I don't remember seeing the top of the building! I could imagine how fighter pilots had blanked out an entire ejection sequence though...things really happen quickly. The automatic sequence occurs 1.5 seconds after ejection, if you are below 7,500 feet MSL (mean sea level), or when the G loads on the seat drop below 3 if you are above 7,500 feet.

My newly-issued card read; "Altitude Training, Air Compression and Oxygen Tolerance, Type 1 Mod, Visual Problems with Demonstrations and Ejection Seat Training, Martin Baker SJU-5/6 INDOC LEH DYNAMIC." I was physiologically ready to fly.

F/A-18As of VFA-132 'Privateers' were fired upon by Russian-made SA-2 Guideline missiles during OPERATION EL DORADO CANYON, the punitive airstrikes against Libya, fortunately they all missed their targets.

An F/A-18A Hornet of VMFA-314 aboard USS CORAL SEA during operations against Libya on 14 April 1986.

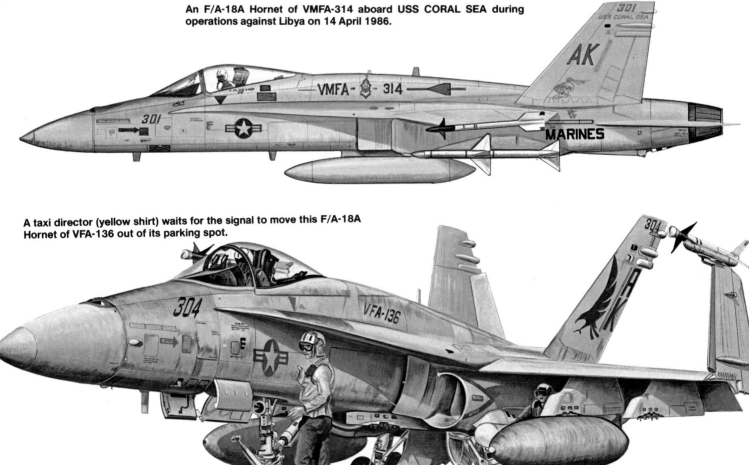

A taxi director (yellow shirt) waits for the signal to move this F/A-18A Hornet of VFA-136 out of its parking spot.

# Heads-Up Display Symbology

**(NAV MASTER MODE)**                    **BASIC FLIGHT DATA**

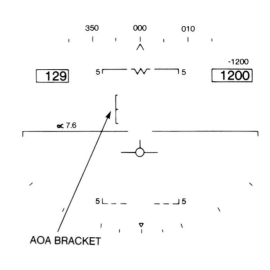

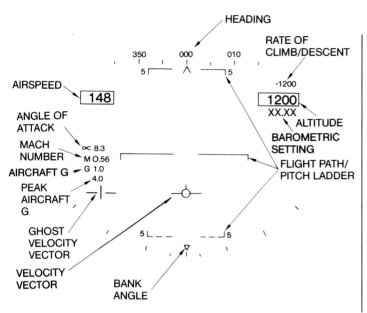

**GEAR UP**                    **GEAR DOWN**

## Navigation Controls And Indicators

## DAY TWO

As a warmup for my ride in the F/A-18B, I was scheduled for an hour of simulator time to get familiar with the Hornet cockpit, which is the most up-to-date of all American military cockpits. My simulator "hop" was scheduled for 1145, but we showed up at VFA-106 at 0900 to get acquainted and to talk to some of the pilots about flying the Hornet. VFA-106's complement is made up of one-third Marines and two-thirds Sailors, including enlisted and officers, aviators and ground personnel. All of the instructor pilots have previous fleet experience. Most of the Marines have come from F-4 Phantom squadrons, while most of the Navy pilots have come from A-7 Corsair II squadrons.

Before climbing into the simulator, I got CAPT C.R. Hull off in the corner and asked him how he felt about flying the Hornet. He was understandably enthusiastic and very articulate. His comments follow;

___*"The first thing you discover about the Hornet is that the cockpit was designed by a pilot, for a pilot. When you first start flying it, you think there is too much information on the HUD (Heads Up Display). In addition to the HUD, you have three solid-state DDIs (Digital Display Indicators). One of these is used principally for navigation, while the other two are used to manage the systems in the airplane. During an air-to-air engagement, we will fly with the HUD repeater on the left DDI, since when your nose is pointed at the sun all the information on the HUD disappears. In the air-to-ground mission, we will have the stores display on the left DDI. That gives us a constant update on what we have left on the airplane, and the status of each weapon. The radar display is on the right DDI.*

*The other great thing about the Hornet design is the hands on throttle and stick, or HOTAS concept, which allows you to use every combat system in the airplane without removing your hands from either the throttle or the stick. That allows us to concentrate on the number one priority for a fighter pilot...looking out the window. There is so much information available on the HUD and those DDIs that it is a real temptation to have your head buried in the cockpit all the time. Once you are engaged and start turning, the Hornet is a real simple airplane to fly and fight.*

*There are things the airplane does not do as well as we would like. For instance, it has a relatively straight wing, and a large bubble canopy. That makes for a lot of drag, and with a non-movable intake ramp, our top speed is limited to about Mach 1.8. (Contrasted to the F-4, which was better than Mach 2 when new or the F-15, which is a Mach 2.5 airplane. Projected Soviet adversaries would probably be in those same speed ranges.) Of course, that's not a number we deal with much in our mission. As you know, there are two kinds of speed. There is Mach, and there is "Q". Mach number applies when you are at high altitude, while "Q" is the aerodynamic pressure encountered in the denser air down low. Down there we can get indicated airspeeds of 725 knots with a clean airplane. On an actual mission, whether it is power projection off the front end of the boat or from an austere airfield like the Marines operate from, we will start hanging stuff on the airplane and degrading our speed. That puts us behind some of the other modern airplanes...ours and theirs in speed, but the thing the Hornet does best is turn.*

*As an example, in the 330 to 380 knot range, the Hornet has a fairly flat lift curve. This gives us some pretty neat options in a fight. We can vary our airspeed within this range, while maintaining the same turn rate. Assuming we start the fight with a head-on pass, if we are fighting the Belgian Congo, or someone who has a rear-quarter only capability, (the ability to fire at the enemy only from the rear) you might make it a two-circle fight with the guy. You fly up towards the fast end, but your nose still gets pointed up at him at the same rate. Because we are going faster, we are able to get more separation for missile launch parameters across the circle. If you are fighting a more sophisticated weapons platform, and you are worried about him getting his nose pointed at you for a shot, you can slow it down and really tighten your circle for a one circle fight. There are not many pilots or airplanes that are going to stick with the average Hornet in that situation! The place where we really excel, and beat all other airplanes, is on the slow end...below 200 knots."*

*—*

When I asked him at what speed the airplane "departed", (in more familiar parlance, that would be "stalled") he said that it would depart at any airspeed, but that it could actually be flown down to zero airspeed! This is so far removed from the normal way in which we think of conventional airplanes, that it takes some getting used to. He tried to explain it in the following manner:

*—"The airplane really doesn't care about airspeed. What it doesn't like are exceptionally high angles of attack. (AOA is measured in units, or degrees, of "Alfa") Once you get beyond 35 Alfa, you are not turning as well as you were before. The lift curve goes up at a pretty constant rate until you reach 35, then it declines rather abruptly. Now, you can go to 60 Alfa, and the jet really doesn't care, as a rule. It won't really "depart"...you can drive it around stalled...though there are some areas of instability... for instance, between 40 and 50 Alfa. Of course, we don't normally operate there. Our HUD airspeed only goes down to 48 knots, and you can fly it that slow, with the Alfa at zero, or you can fly it at 48 knots with the Alfa at 55...it is controllable in all of those regimes. The F-16 is an unbelievable turning airplane above 200 knots, but then they have an Alfa limiter, and when they get slow, that's when we can beat them. The F-15...as old as it is...is a great turning airplane that can fly slow. Neither one of them has the maneuvering flaps we have, but the bad news is...if either of them don't like what's going on and they can ever get the lateral separation on us, they have a much better chance of leaving the fight than we do. We assume the bad guys are building airplanes with similar capabilities. Of course, the way airplanes perform today, unless you meet 180 degrees out, going as fast you can, nobody is able to leave the fight! You have to stay in there until someone gets shot down."—*

I wondered what good all that close-in turning capability was going to do when today's radar guided missiles were BVR (beyond visual range) and were being fired from twenty-five miles away.

*—"Just about every scenario that we have planned for is going to call for VID (Visual Identification). So we are definitely looking at shooting missiles at seven to eight miles maximum, and one and a half miles minimum. We carry the AIM-7 Sparrow, which is a BVR missile, and if we get a cleared to fire from higher authority, we can launch it at twenty-five miles. (The way he said that made it sound highly unlikely that such permission would be forthcoming.) The AIM-9 we carry is the same Sidewinder we have had for years, except it is better. It can track a lesser heat source, which means it is an all-aspect missile. The gunsight in the Hornet is the best of all contemporary fighters. It tells you exactly where your bullets are going in relation to the target. It computes your speed, attitude, G, bullet time of flight, and takes additional information off of the radar locks. The bottom line is, if you put the pipper on his airplane and shoot, he is going to get a bullet in his airplane, unless he changes position in the time it takes for your bullet to get to him. I am not saying it is magic...it's not a death beam, or anything...but unless his airplane changes direction during the bullet time of flight, it is going to hit him.—*

*— Our training is not geared to turning fights, but when you get into a turning fight, it usually degrades to a slower airspeed, which in turn means less separation and less likelihood of shooting a missile. That makes this gun even more valuable. We train to shoot targets in front of us, and the preferred missile is the AIM-9 because it is basically a "launch and leave" weapon (it tracks the heat from the target's engine). The AIM-7 is radar guided, but you must maintain the radar lock while the missile is in the air...and that can be a long, long time. Fifteen seconds can be an eternity in an air-to-air battle. The reason we train this way is that we train for multiple-bogeys, and you don't want to be slow when you have to contend with more than one enemy airplane.*

*There is absolutely no difference in the way the airplane feels at 650 knots or at 48 knots. It took me about six hops to get used to that. (In a normal airplane, the controls get "hard" as the airplane goes faster and the aerodynamic pressures increase.) The sound levels don't change with increases in airspeed either, but there are subtle cues that you start to pick up as you fly the airplane more. The cues are related to Alpha. A "buzz" on the airframe starts about 10 and is really noticeable at 12. If you are looking back over your shoulder, you'll see the tails flapping. (Early models of the Hornet developed cracks in the tail attachment points which resulted in a strengthening modification for the entire fleet.) Visual cues include how far the leading or trailing edge flaps are down, (they are automatic) and in spite of what I said about no difference in feel, after awhile the seat of your pants will tell you where you are. It is the easiest airplane to fly that I have ever flown. I cannot imagine an airplane being any easier to fly than the Hornet. The only problem you have is managing the systems, because of all the information that is generated.*

*You can depart the airplane, if you are really ham-handed, but even at that this is a forgiving airplane. It will usually give you a couple of seconds of "heads-up" before departure. Now, if you ignore it, it's going to take you for a ride."—*

I had heard stories about the flight control computer "taking the airplane away" from ham-handed pilots who were about to do something stupid. I wondered about that, especially since the Hornet pilots I had talked to referred to the airplane as a distinct personality...not as having a personality, but rather actually being a personality. They kept coming up with quotes like; "If you do something the airplane doesn't like...". I wondered if I stuck the stick in a corner, and stomped full opposite rudder, if the computer would take the airplane away from me.

*—"Not necessarily. The airplane would probably just give you those inputs. Sometimes the computer may say; "Hey, I'm not sure what this guy wants, but I'll give him a cross-control." But it never says; "Hey, this guy is going to hurt himself." It will keep*

**'OD' O'Donnell demonstrates the vertical performance his F/A-18 as he goes 'over the top'. (Author)**

*doing exactly what you ask, with one exception. If you get extremely slow...let's say you are flying a loop...and the nose stops tracking as you go over the top. The computer doesn't know what's going on, so it tries to trim the airplane for 1 G flight, which will create a problem. But that is not going to happen to anybody who has flown the airplane more than about five times.*

*The Hornet is unquestionably the best multi-mission fighter in the world. There is not going to be an airplane that bombs better than this one in my lifetime, and there is not going to be an airplane that turns better than this one until we get one with wings that go the wrong way and has vectored thrust."—*

Encouraged by the promise of a supersonic jet that is easy to fly, Marty Wilcox and I headed for the simulator for my hour of fun and games. These simulators are kept busy, and the previous flyer was just stepping out of the cockpit as we walked into the room. The simulator room was large, noisy, and had that sterile feeling of high-tech artificiality...perfect for a simulator environment. The operators told us to go ahead and man the airplane...they hadn't shut the

engines down. I gingerly climbed in and settled into what felt like a waterbed; it was. The simulator cannot duplicate the gut-squeezing feeling of 6 Gs, but it can give you a gentle thump in the butt with it's water-filled seat cushion that is supposed to give you a sensory cue.

Marty began my cockpit briefing with the left console, which contains such items as the oxygen control panel, communications control panels, fuel management system, ground power system, and the twin throttles. The throttles have enough switches, buttons, and levers on them to require a two-hour checkout themselves. They are half of the HOTAS system which makes the Hornet such a great pilot's airplane. They contain Communications buttons for two radios and the intercom, speed brake, designator controller, radar antenna elevation, flare/chaff switch, exterior lights, RAID/FLIR FOV select, ATC engage/disengage, and finger lifts to enable after-burner selection while on the ground. The other half of this dynamic duo is the control stick, which contains the air/ground weapons release button, the weapons select switch, a four position sensor control switch, a pitch and roll trim switch, the trigger, an undesignate nosewheel steering button, and the paddle switch on the lower front of the stick which has multiple functions, including nosewheel steering disengage, autopilot disengage, and G-limiter override. I was reminded of the F-15 Eagle pilot who had told me that learning to use all of these switches and buttons was what they called "playing the piccollo" and required constant practice to stay sharp. In the

**'Roman 86' flight, with LT Bill Hedstrom and the author in the F/A-18B and LT John O'Donnell in the F/A-18A single-seater. ('Shooter' Shot)**

split-second furor of an air-to-air battle, with multiple bogies (also called a "furball"), HOTAS is a big advantage...if you practice enough to develop virtuosity.

The instrument panel is not an instrument panel at all, in the traditional sense. There are only seven "old fashioned" instruments on the panel, including the backup artificial horizon, and they are stuck down in the lower right hand corner...almost as an afterthought. Dominating the panel are the three DDIs. The DDIs (Digital Display Indicators) are really Cathode Ray Tubes...TV screens, that display the hundreds of bits of information needed to manage the Hornet's systems. The communications panel (AKA Up Front Control Panel) is right under the HUD. The placement of the Up Front Control Panel, right in front of the pilot at the top of the panel, is a major improvement over military cockpits of the fifties and sixties, which had the radios on one of the side consoles. In the F/A-18, you can change radio frequencies with a flick of your eyes. Naturally, this is important in a combat situation, but it is even more valuable in the more mundane, and often-encountered, world of instrument flying. In addition to the controls for the two comm radios, Identification, Friend or Foe (IFF), Tactical Air Navigation (TACAN), and emissions control, the Upfront Control Panel also programs the Inertial Navigation System (INS).

The radio system includes both UHF and VHF, and voice transmissions from both can be enciphered for security. The IFF is better known in the civilian world as a transponder. The Hornet transponder can be operated in four modes plus a crypto mode. The inertial navigation system provides dead reckoning navigation without any external navigational aids. It does this by detecting motion through three accelerometers and two gyros. Navigational information is presented on the middle DDI, and includes an Horizontal Situation Indicator (HSI) or waypoint data (latitude, longitude, magnetic variation, wind direction, and speed). This DDI is surrounded by twenty buttons and four knobs for controlling the various navigational functions, one of which is a moving map display for pure "look out the window and compare what you see with your map" navigation. The difference here is that the Hornet's navigation system is telling you exactly where you are on that map.

The right console contains the interior lights panel, a map and data case, and several blank panels.

An F/A-18A of VFA-25 assigned to the USS CONSTELLATION (CV-64) on the transit ramp at Davis-Monthan AFB, Arizona on 31 March 1984. (Brian Rogers via Norm Taylor)

# THE FLIGHT

Our flight was given the call sign of "Roman 86", and consisted of LT Bill Hedstrom and I in the lead F/A-18B, with LT John O'Donnell flying number two in an F/A-18A. Hedstrom is a veteran Naval Aviator, with over 1,000 hours and three cruises in the A-7 Corsair II. He had flown the Hornet 800 hours at the time of our flight. O'Donnell was also a Corsair veteran, with 900 hours, including support of the Grenada invasion and operations over Lebanon. O.D. had flown the F/A-18 a total of 700 hours. Our briefing was at 1330 and was held in one of the many small rooms off of the long hallway that runs the length of one of the large hangars at NAS Cecil. As the East Coast RAG for the Hornet, VFA-106 flies dozens of sorties each day, requiring several individual briefing/flight planning rooms for students and their instructors. The ready room is a constant beehive of activity, with instructors coming and going continually. VFA-106's Hornets run almost from dawn til dusk.

Modern jet fighters are concentrated bundles of pure performance. You really are living out there on the edge when you fly these supersonic marvels, even those (like the Hornet) that are "easy" to fly. The energy required to give them their spectacular performance is tremendous. In the case of the Hornet, it is generated by the twin GE F-404 engines, which convert a finite supply of jet fuel to knots, or Gs, or altitude. Fighter pilots learn early that fuel is an overriding concern, since their airplanes are capable of using what they carry faster than most other types of airplanes. One of the essential preflight tasks is planning the required fuel burn for that mission. Hedstrom had drawn a diagram that resembled a ladder, each rung representing a milestone in our flight, with his calculation of fuel burn for each leg penciled in. Each aspect of the mission was discussed, including the frequencies and call signs for the control agencies we would be talking to, procedures for the maneuvers, and how much fuel should be remaining after each segment. Our takeoff was scheduled for 1500, with a proposed recovery time of 1630...or "whenever we run out of gas". Both airplanes had been reported "up" and after a final run-through of the photographic views I wanted, we headed for the personal equipment room to get dressed for the flight.

The Anti-G suit, or "speed jeans", as it is sometimes called, is one of the more valuable items in a fighter pilot's wardrobe. I thought it must also be one of the more uncomfortable, as I snapped, zipped, and twisted mine into place. The suit is like a pair of leggings with a built-in girdle, and it is attached to the airplane with a thick hose. The bladders on the suit inflate as you pull Gs, squeezing your calves, thighs, and stomach to defeat the gravitational pooling of blood in your lower extremities. The more Gs you pull, the harder the suit squeezes, and if you wear it tight to begin with, it is that much more effective when the Gs come on.

The torso harness, which contains the attachment fittings for the lap belt and parachute risers, is also uncomfortable. In fact, it is the torso harness that turns your walk into a waddle. But when you put on the last piece of gear...the LPU, you really feel like you look as though you should be waddling! And this was a peace-time mission. Going to war, you also put on a survival vest, knife, and gun! (Then have someone carry you out to the airplane.) There is no way to look like Tom Cruise when you are trussed up like this...which is probably why all those guys in "Top Gun" unbuckled everything before they walked in front of the cameras. However, I did note that the guys who are doing this full time seem to have developed a way of disguising the fact that walking with all this stuff on is an unnatural act.

Trying to look as nonchalant as possible, I followed Bill out to the airplane, and while he did his preflight walk-around, I unlimbered the cameras. There are twenty-three separate areas on the preflight check of the aircraft exterior, each with three to six items that are supposed to be checked. When you have flown as many missions in the Hornet as Bill Hedstrom, the preflight can be completed in a few minutes. But even after you climb the ladder, before you can sit down, a further sixteen items on the ejection seat must be checked! He completed all that...for both seats...and beckoned me to climb aboard.

The Hornet has its own internal boarding ladder, which means one less ground (or deck) support piece of equipment. Once up the ladder, getting into the cockpit was fairly easy. The big, clamshell canopy is opened high enough to allow you to step on the seat and get in without bending yourself double. Your attachments to the airplane include two leg restraint lines each leg, two lap belt snap fittings, two parachute riser/inertial reel snap fittings, G-suit, and oxygen/comm lines. That is pretty much the same routine as with the older F-4 Phantom. The difference here is that the canopy line is down around your waist, instead of at shoulder level, which means that the plane captain can help you get everything in place. In the Phantom, there just is not much room for anyone to help you with that stuff. Our plane captain had me buckled in in what seemed like record time.

There are no external power carts on the Hornet flight line because the F/A-18 can be started with internal power only. That is another advantage when a quick deployment is necessary. Hedstrom started the internal APU on battery power and when it was running, he punched the start button for the right engine. The engine spooled up immediately and, as it passed through 60% rpm, the crank switch cycled off and the generator came on line. With the right engine running normal hydraulics were available for the brakes. When the left engine was running the APU shut down. Bill checked the controls, with the plane captain on the ground verifying that they were doing what they were expected to do for the control inputs. Then he checked the inertial navigation system, radar, wings unfolded and locked, flaps and trim set at takeoff, and set the fuel quantity gage at bingo ("bingo" is fuel required to return to base with the specified reserve). He cycled the air refueling probe, launch bar, and tail hook, set the barometric altimeter at the pressure setting being advertised on the recorded airport information message and turned on the

An F/A-18A-16-MC (BuNo 162467) of VMFA-531 at Carswell AFB, Texas on 11 October 1986. The 'Gray Ghosts' were commissioned as a Hornet squadron in July of 1983 with LTCOL Jim Lucas as Commanding Officer. (Brian Rogers via Norm Taylor)

radar altimeter.

Our wingman had finished his preliminaries first and I saw him taxi out of his parking spot, proceed to an open area on the ramp, where he turned and waited for us to catch up and take the lead. Our plane captain finished his external checks, and relayed Bill's signal to pull the chocks to the rest of the ground crew. When they were clear, he waved us out and as we began to roll, he saluted us on our way.

We rolled to the end of the parking line, where the ordnance crew waited to pull the safety pins on our six MK 76 practice bombs. It was a warm day, and Bill said he intended to leave the canopy open until we were ready to depart. I wondered aloud why he didn't just turn up the air conditioning, and he replied that the air conditioning system was designed for the single seater, and was really not effective when you were on the ground. We kept our hands in sight as the safety pins were pulled from our bombs, and as I watched the crew scurry around under the jet, I felt that sense of isolation peculiar to people in totally different jobs who work in close proximity... or maybe it was just the noise level, which mandated ear protection for everyone, and removed the ability to communicate normally. Or maybe it was being in a jet... this jet, which is at the leading edge of our military technology, and is flown by a very select cadre of young professionals, that gave me a sense, however temporary, of being privileged.

As we sat in the runup area awaiting takeoff clearance, Bill went through the final pre-takeoff checklist, which appeared on the right hand DDI. The canopy was now closed, shutting out even the muted roar of jet engines. The predominant sound was our breathing, amplified by the oxygen masks, and made ubiquitous because of the hot mike mode of Intercom operation. The last item on that checklist was "SEAT ARM", and Bill finally said; "O.K., lets arm up our seats." I reached down to the right side of the seat and squeezed the locking lever and rotated the handle down.

I looked up to see a ghost grey A-7 flash across the runway threshold and touch down in a cloud of burning rubber blue smoke. The controller cleared us into position and hold as the A-7 continued down the runway and lifted off on his touch and go. We lined up for a section takeoff, with O.D. on our left side, slightly behind us. In normal cruise, or parade formations, the wingman assumes a position behind and 45 degrees off the leader, but in formation takeoffs, the wingman assumes an acute position at line up. Bill looked over at O.D. and they exchanged "thumbs ups" to indicate

that each had looked over the other's airplane to confirm that speed brakes were retracted, flaps were set, all panels were closed, there were no fluids leaking, safety pins were pulled, rudders were toed in, and the launch bars were retracted. Bill looked down the runway, and when the controller cleared us for takeoff, he lifted his left arm, then lowered it and advanced the throttles into afterburner.

There is just no feeling in the world like the acceleration of the new jet fighters. Within 2500 feet we had accelerated to 150 knots and were flying. Once off the ground, the acceleration increases, and you cannot delay gear retraction for very long for fear of exceeding the gear transition speed. Bill nodded once, and I saw the gear handle come up. I looked over to see our wingman's gear coming up simultaneously. Another nod, and all four throttles came back out of afterburner, throwing us against our shoulder harnesses. The little box on the DDI told me we were doing 250 knots, which is the speed limit below 10,000 feet under civilian control. We would keep it at 250 while heading for the low-level route to the target area.

The flight turned west, then gradually back to the south-southeast, heading for the Palatka 1 Military Operating Area (MOA), and the Rodman Target, 75 miles south of Cecil. We remained at this relatively sedate speed, and at least 1,000 feet above ground as we headed south and I fired off frame after frame of pictures of O.D. while he moved back, forward, up, down, and under us. As we approached the beginning of our low level run into the target, Hedstrom switched over to Pinecastle Control, the military sector controller who would monitor all tactical traffic in the area.

According to the little altitude box on the DDI, we were now down at 300 feet AGL, and our airspeed was 500 knots. I was fascinated by the display of those numbers, because they kept changing to indicate changes in our actual speed, altitude and movement. According to the old analog pressure instruments on the lower right hand corner of the panel, we were rock-steady at 300 feet and 500 knots. The really sensitive instrument readings on the DDI said we were bouncing up and down from 290 to 310 feet, and doing anywhere from 490 to 510 knots, with the VSI above the altitude reading reflecting the rate of change instantly. Straight and level over the ground the radar altimeter was working and this was indicated by an "R" to the right of the altitude readout. (Later, when we began vertical work and the radar altimeter antenna was pointed away from the ground, the pressure altimeter took over and a barometric pressure reading appeared under the altitude readout to indicate this.) The digital accelerometer was recording every bump in the warm, humid late afternoon air, and I could occasionally catch a glimpse of ghost-like condensation trails off our wingman's airplane.

Florida contains some of the most stark contrasts an aviator will see. You can go from the glitz and glamour of Miami to the absolute wilderness of the Everglades in minutes. You can fly by Cape Canaveral, the gateway to the future, and within minutes be over land so desolate that a gravel road represents a major mark of civilization. We were within 50 miles of Orlando, one of the fastest-growing metropolitan areas in the country, and yet, looking down at the countryside flashing past our wings, it was hard to imagine anything more rural. The pine forests were interrupted by an occasional dirt road, or sharecropper's trailer but as we approached the Restricted Area of the target, even those signs of civilization disappeared.

Pinecastle Control handed us off to Rodman Target, and Bill said; "O.K., here we go!" We circled the target in a tight, right orbit and when he had the target lined up, Bill pulled up, rolled over, pulled the nose down and put the pipper on the target. He kept it there as he rolled wings-level and dove. I could feel the minute corrections he was making with the controls to keep the target reference box on the HUD marching towards the target. When it intersected, he pickled off three bombs and I was crushed by the 6.5 G pull-off. I tried to look back over my right shoulder to see where the bombs hit, but couldn't quite manage to get twisted around far enough with all those Gs working on me. The target observer called three bulls-eyes, then we heard O.D. call; "Two's in hot!" as he began his dive on the target.

The tremendous agility of the Hornet allows you to keep your speed up and still work close to the target, but the price you pay is an almost constant G load on your body as you are rolling, diving and pulling. The advantage of this is that it makes you a tough target for the opposition to track, and since your bomb runs are so close together, they will be encouraged to keep their heads down anyway. O.D. had not had a chance to drop bombs in over two months, but all three of his bombs were scored as direct hits by the target observer. I immediately remembered Hull telling me that there would not be a bomber better than this one in this century. Our next run resulted in two hits and a hung bomb. Hedstrom recycled the armament switches and told O.D. to go high while we made one more run on the target in an attempt to get rid of the hung bomb. But all we got out of that run was another dose of Gs. The bomb was stubbornly hung, and would remain so throughout the next series of maneuvers, which involved vertical maneuvers.

Some of the most impressive airplane photography shows the airplane going straight up, or straight down. The only way to get these pictures is a formation loop. Our first vertical maneuver had us starting straight up, then O.D. would roll away from us so that I could get a shot of the belly of his airplane in the vertical position. Bill called for afterburner and as I felt the extra push, the stick came back and we headed up. Since I was concentrating on picture-taking, I could not tell how we recovered after O.D. had rolled and pulled away from us. I was impressed with how slow it felt as we came over the top, and how quickly the two Hornets rejoined for our second maneuver, a formation loop. On this attempt, O.D. got slightly sucked (fell behind) and disappeared under our wing. He reappeared as we came over the top and started down. We passed the lead to him for our third attempt, and started up almost line-abreast. As we approached the inverted horizontal, we became acute and lost sight of O.D. Bill observed the cardinal precept of formation flying as soon as he lost sight of the leader. He said; "I'm outta here!", and rolled away from O.D.

Hedstrom was maintaining a rigid mission profile and a quick check of our fuel state told him it was time to move on. The next segment of this mission was something unusual for these pilots. We would rendezvous with a 1950s vintage Navy trainer for some original formation photography.

Roy Stafford owns a T-34B, the first airplane in which all naval aviators, from the late fifties to the mid-seventies, soloed. Known as the "Teeney Weeney", the Beechcraft Mentor enjoyed a long and fruitful career as the Navy's primary trainer. It's popularity is not limited to the military. Though less than 1,200 were built by Beech, it has become one of the most popular civilian-owned ex-military aircraft, with the price of a well-restored T-34 equal to a new Bonanza. Roy's T-34 has a 285 HP engine, which gives it a big performance increase over the original 225 HP version. When he proposed this formation, we hoped that the extra speed of the 285 version of the Teeney Weeney would enable the Hornets to stay with it without falling out of the sky.

Our briefing with Roy had consisted of a proposed rendezvous time, altitude, and direction of flight once we were joined up. The F/A-18 has both VHF and UHF radios, so we were able to agree on a common VHF radio frequency for the rendezvous. (The military almost always uses UHF exclusively, while civilians use VHF, making it impossible to communicate air-to-air via radio.) Another difference between military and civilian procedures is radio identification. Civilians usually use the aircraft identification when speaking on the radio. For example, "Beech eight charlie november" is how you would refer to yourself on the radio if your aircraft registration number was N8CN, which is what Roy's registration number is. On the other hand, military aircraft are always assigned a tactical call sign, which may be computer-generated for ease of phonetic understanding or because it may have a particular significance. "Roman 86" was assigned to us because VFA-106 are "The Gladiators", and this was sortie 86. The unofficial tactical call signs made so popular by the movie "Top Gun" are nothing more than nom-de-guerres...nicknames...by which fighter pilots call each other...on the ground or in the air. They provide an easy shorthand for those in the know. Roy had picked "Shadow" for his call sign.

Hedstrom called twice; "Shadow, this is Roman 86, over." Within seconds Roy had answered, giving his position as just east of Palatka at 6,500 feet. Roy's Mentor is painted in 1950's Navy trainer Yellow, a scheme designed to be seen from long distance. My T-34 is painted the same way, as are several of those we fly with, and it is still not that easy to spot from a couple of miles away...unless you have the eyes of a twenty-five year old fighter pilot. Bill called "Tally-ho, 10 o'clock low!" I looked out the left side, and there he was, about 2 miles away. The rendezvous was remarkably quick and smooth, considering the speed differential. When Hedstrom called "Tally-ho", Roy put his nose down to pick up the 170 knots we had agreed upon. We figured that would give him a rate of descent of about 500 feet per minute, and give us five or six minutes to formate on him.

Captain Mike "Shooter" Shot, USMC, another Hornet pilot from VFA-106, was Roy's back-seater for this mission, and as we slid into position on his right wing, Mike fired off a couple of dozen frames. Then Bill slid under Roy, while O.D. stayed on his right wing so we could photograph their formation.

It is one thing to have a pilot tell you that his airplane is the best in the world at what it does, (most pilots do) but when he can show you, almost in the same breath...well, that is memorable! When C.R. Hull told me that the Hornet was at its best when the fight got slow, and that it was controllable at very high angles of attack, well...it just didn't mean that much to me. But when we pulled in on Roy's wing, I began to be impressed. The Hornet's flight control computer programmed the leading and trailing edge flaps to compensate for the slower airspeed and higher AOA, and as nearly as I could tell, the airplane did not mush like most airplanes do when they sense that

**The author (right) with LT Bill Hedstrom on the flightline at NAS Cecil Field, Florida after returning from his orientation flight in the F/A-18B Hornet.**

A line up of F/A-18As of Marine Fighter Attack Squadron 115. VMFA-115 is one of the latest Marine Corps squadrons to convert to the Hornet. (McDonnell Douglas)

they are flying too slow. And when Bill pulled up and rolled over the top of their formation, at 160 knots, so I could take a picture straight down, I was goggle-eyed! (Roy said later, quite unequivocally; "If you had tried that in a Phantom, you'd be a dead man!")

Our plan was to fly up the St. Johns River after we left Roy, making a pass over downtown Jacksonville to get some landmarks in the background. The hung bomb on our airplane made that seem like a bad idea. (Even a 25 pound practice bomb could ruin your whole day if it landed on your head.) The hung bomb also precluded an overhead approach with the traditional 4 G pitchout to downwind for landing. (If the bomb had come off on pitchout, it would probably have been slung onto the flight line.) We flew a straight-in approach, touching down on 36 right just an hour and fifteen minutes

after leaving our parking spot. After getting the safety pin inserted in the bomb, we taxied to the fuel pit and hot refueled before parking.

Reflecting on my encounter with the F/A-18, if I had to summarize a description, I would say it is "state of the art". I know that that has become a hackneyed cliche, and that is unfortunate, because every aspect of the Hornet represents the best of current technology. The engines put out a tremendous amount of power for their size and weight and they are reliable. The airframe can do things that defy conventional aircraft design parameters. The avionics are futuristic. The weapons system makes aces of ordinary pilots. It is easy to maintain. About the only thing it isn't is cheap, but then, neither are Ferraris!

**The deck crew of USS CONSTELLATION (CV-64) conduct a FOD walk down prior to beginning flight operations with F/A-18s of VFA-25. (McDonnell Douglas)**

(Above) An F/A-18A (BuNo 161967) of the newest Marine Hornet squadrons VMFA-251, on the ramp at MCAS Beaufort, South Carolina on 16 September 1986. The squadron's lightning bolt unit marking is painted in Light Gray on the tail and is barely visible. (Norman E. Taylor)

(Left) CDR Craig Langbehn and LTJG Russ Bird of VFA-113 return from a target near MCAS Yuma, Arizona during late 1983. The 'Stingers' were the first tactical Navy Hornet squadron and converted from the A-7E Corsair II. The subdued squadron insignia is a far cry from the bright 'Bumblebee' that was carried on the Corsair. (Tailhook Photo Service Robert L. Lawson)

(Below) An F/A-18A (BuNo 161952) of VMFA-122 tied down to the ramp at MCAS Beaufort on 16 September 1986. VMFA-122 converted from the F-4J Phantom II to the Hornet. The pilot's tactical call sign 'Cheetah' is painted in Dark Gray on the fuselage side below the canopy. (Norman E. Taylor)

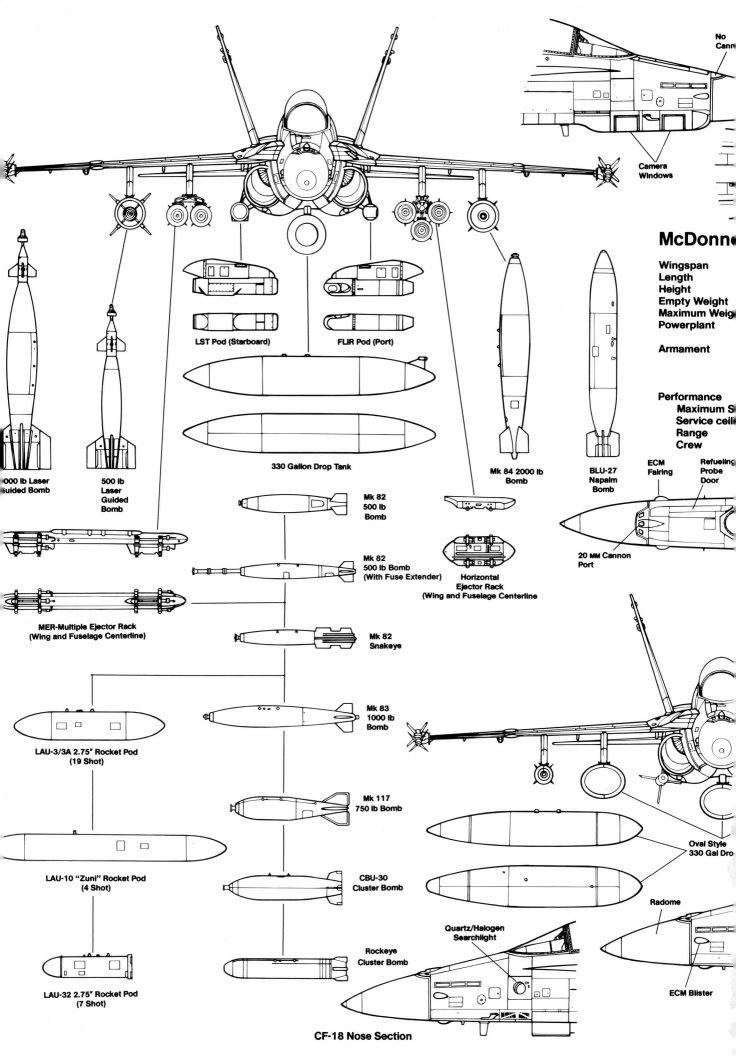

No
Cann

Camera
Windows

**McDonn**

Wingspan
Length
Height
Empty Weight
Maximum Weig
Powerplant

Armament

Performance
    Maximum S
    Service ceili
    Range
    Crew

LST Pod (Starboard)

FLIR Pod (Port)

Mk 84 2000 lb
Bomb

BLU-27
Napalm
Bomb

000 lb Laser
Guided Bomb

500 lb
Laser
Guided
Bomb

330 Gallon Drop Tank

ECM
Fairing

Refueling
Probe
Door

20 мм Cannon
Port

Mk 82
500 lb
Bomb

Mk 82
500 lb Bomb
(With Fuse Extender)

Horizontal
Ejector Rack
(Wing and Fuselage Centerline

MER-Multiple Ejector Rack
(Wing and Fuselage Centerline)

Mk 82
Snakeye

Mk 83
1000 lb
Bomb

LAU-3/3A 2.75" Rocket Pod
(19 Shot)

Mk 117
750 lb Bomb

Oval Style
330 Gal Dro

LAU-10 "Zuni" Rocket Pod
(4 Shot)

CBU-30
Cluster Bomb

Radome

Quartz/Halogen
Searchlight

Rockeye
Cluster Bomb

LAU-32 2.75" Rocket Pod
(7 Shot)

ECM Blister

**CF-18 Nose Section**

**RF-18 Nose Section**

Camera Windows

Martin Baker Ejection Seat

Formation Strip Lights

# Douglas F/A-18B Hornet

36 feet 3 inches
56 feet
15 feet 3½ inches
23,500 pounds
49,724 pounds
Two 16,000 lbst GE F-404-GE-400

One M-61 20mm cannon
Nine external weapons stations

1,305 mph
50,000 feet
2,165 miles
Two

Open Speed Brake

All Moving Tailplane

GE F404-GE-400 Engines

Speed Brake

LEX (Leading Edge) Extension

ECM Fairings

Flaps

Wing Fold Joint

Aileron

Mk 82 Bomb

AIM 9L Sidewinder

ECM Fairings

Rudder

Tank

Intake

Sparrow Missile

Tail Hook

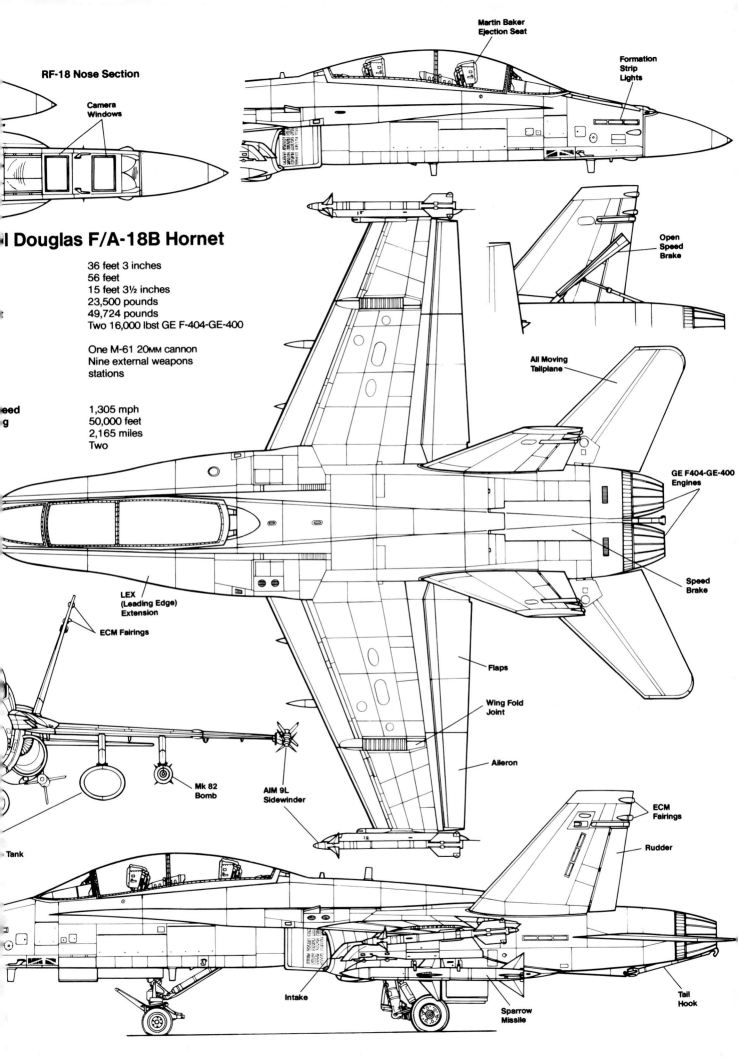

(Above) VMFA-115, based at MCAS Beaufort, South Carolina have changed their tail markings to the larger Eagle shown on this F/A-18A (BuNo 162465) on the ramp at neighboring Shaw AFB, South Carolina on 5 January 1986. (Norman E. Taylor)

(Right) Hornets of three different Marine Squadrons (VMFA-314, VMFA-531, and VMFA-323) practice refueling from a USAF KC-10 Extender tanker. It is common practice for Navy and Marine squadrons to conduct refueling exercises with Air Force tankers. (McDonnell Douglas)

(Below) An F/A-18A (BuNo 162860) of VFA-136 assigned to USS CORAL SEA (CV-43) at Florence, South Carolina on 2 May 1986 has tail markings similar to those used by VFMA-115.
(Norman E. Taylor)

Hornets of the Navy's first reserve F/A-18 squadron, VFA-303 'Golden Hawks', prepare for carrier qualifications. VFA-303, based at NAS Miramar, California won the reserve Tailhook Squadron of the Year award in 1986. (Tailhook Photo Service Robert L. Lawson)

(Left) An F/A-18A of Marine Fighter Attack Squadron 314 (VMFA-314) escorts a Libyan Air Force MiG-25 Foxbat armed with AA-6 'Acrid' long range missiles and AA-8 'Aphid' dog fight missiles over the Mediterranean during 1986. (via Robert F. Dorr)

An F/A-18 of VMFA-323, 'Death Rattlers' touches down aboard USS CORAL SEA during flight operations off the coast of Libya on 18 March 1986. (U.S. Navy)

(Above) An F/A-18 of VMFA-323 coming aboard USS CORAL SEA. During operational deployments, Navy squadrons achieved a 99% boarding rate with the F/A-18 — the best rate ever achieved by a new attack aircraft. (McDonnell Douglas)

(Below) The U.S. Sixth Fleet was continually shadowed by Libyan Soviet-built MiGs, such as this fully armed MiG-25 Foxbat. During the U.S. raid on Libya on 15 April 1986, Hornets flew SAM suppression and top cover missions. (via Mule Holmberg)

(Above) F/A-18 Hornets of VFA-131 'Wildcats' enroute to NAS Cecil Field after the traditional fly-off from USS CORAL SEA upon completion of their Med Cruise and Libyan operations. (McDonnell Douglas)

(Below) During their initial work-up periods with the Hornet VFA-25 pilots flew missions from USS CONSTELLATION (CV-64) with live ordnance. The F/A-18 in the foreground waiting its turn for the waist cat is assigned to the Carrier Air Wing Commander (CAG). (McDonnell Douglas)

(Above) F/A-18A Hornets of VFA-25 'Fist of the Fleet' and VFA-113 'Stingers' aboard USS CONSTELLATION for carrier qualifications prior to their first operational deployment. (McDonnell Douglas)

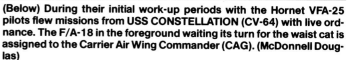

(Below) A VFA-25 Hornet aims for the number three wire aboard USS CONSTELLATION. Landing is not challenge enough for Naval Aviators... they aim for the number three wire, which earns them an 'O.K. Pass' if their approach is handled smoothly. (Tailhook Photo Service Robert L. Lawson)

A VFA-25 Hornet taxies to its parking place aboard 'CONNIE'. Coming aboard is the most difficult challenge in Naval Aviation, but taxiing on a slippery, heaving deck must run a close second. (McDonnell Douglas)

(Below) A Hornet accelerates down the steam catapult. The stabilator position is a pre-selected trim setting to reduce the chances of pilot-induced oscillation (PIO) caused by the tremendous G force sustained by the pilot during the cat shot. (McDonnell Douglas)

(Below) At the high angle of attack (AOA) necessary for a positive climb rate at the end of the cat shot the pilot may lose sight of the horizon. Even under the forces of the cat shot, the pilot must establish a good instrument scan so he can transfer from visual to instrument flight. (McDonnell Douglas)

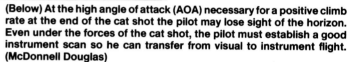

A deck crewman signals the pilot of this Hornet to release his brakes and allow the aircraft to be pulled back far enough to allow the arresting cable to slacken. The hook can then be retracted and the aircraft taxied forward. (McDonnell Douglas)

On glideslope, just seconds from touchdown, this VFA-113 pilot has received the 'cut' signal from the LSO. As soon as the Hornet touches down, he will go to full power until the arresting gear is engaged. (McDonnell Douglas)

(Above) Three early production F/A-18A Hornets of VMFA-314 'Black Knights' enroute to their home based at MCAS El Toro, California. (McDonnell Douglas)

(Below) Hornets of VFA-132 'Privateers' enroute to the target range. VFA-132 took part in the Libya raid of 1986. During the raid the Libyans fired SA-2, SA-3, SA-6, and SA-8 missiles, none of which hit their targets. The F/A-18s carried AGM-88 HARM radar homing missiles which hit their targets. (Tailhook Photo Service Robert L. Lawson)

The Navy's newest F/A-18 squadron is VFA-15 'Valions'. The normal Gray camouflage scheme is accented by Black trim on the tails. The AIM-9L Sidewinders on the wingtips are Blue bodied inert weapons. (McDonnell Douglas)

An F/A-18A of VFA-192 'Golden Dragons', who recently turned in their A-7E Corsair IIs for F/A-18s. The 'Dragons' are home based at NAS Lemoore, California. (McDonnell Douglas)

This flight of McDonnell Douglas aircraft points up a problem the Marines will have for some time. The F/A-18 and AV-8B are flown by active squadrons, while the Reserves fly the A-4 and F-4 complicating logistics and training. (McDonnell Douglas)

An RF/A-18A reconnaissance aircraft carries a camera pallet in place of the nose mounted cannon. The pallet carries two cameras or one camera and an infrared scanner which are compatible with TARPS, the Navy tactical air reconnaissance pod. (McDonnell Douglas)

The 500th F/A-18 was delivered to the Marines in May of 1987. COL Robert Pappas, Commanding Officer of VMFA-451, accepted the Hornet for VMFA-451 and ferried it to MCAS Beaufort, S.C. (McDonnell Douglas)

The first F/A-18C takes off from the McDonnell factory in September of 1987, with company test pilot Glen Larson at the controls. The F/A-18C has a faster, higher capacity computer, new radar jammer, and is capable of carrying the advanced medium range AAM (AMRAAM) and infrared Maverick. (McDonnell Douglas)

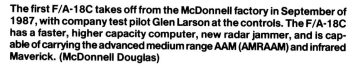

Seven F/A-18As and one F/A-18B from an early production block of air-craft (which were not modified with heavy duty carrier landing gear) were issued to the Blue Angels in late 1986. These aircraft had been used for pilot training and land operations. (McDonnel Douglas)

The Blue Angels are Naval Air Training Command's (NATC) most valu-able public relations and recruiting asset. They fly an aircraft a potential Naval Aviator can aspire to if he wins his Wings of Gold.

The Blue Angels fly over the Silver Strand near NAS North Island, San Diego. The Blue Angels' Hornets are modified with a smoke generating system and a new seat harness to keep the pilot in place during nega-tive G maneuvers. (McDonnell Douglas)

The Blues received their first Hornet in late 1986 and began practicing the following January for the 1987 show season. The Blue Angels fly a hectic schedule and are away from home more than if they were deployed at sea. (Shinichi Ohtaki)

**The Blue Angels perform an echelon turn at low altitude. (Shinichi Ohtaki)**

# FOREIGN HORNETS

Hot on the heels of the formation of its partnership with McDonnell Douglas, Northrop announced it would begin a major sales campaign for the export version of the F-18. At first hesitant to link it directly with the McDonnell Douglas F-18, Northrop considered naming the YF-17 derivative the "Cobra 2", but settled, temporarily, on the cryptic designation "LBV" (for "land-based version"). The Pentagon had no such compunctions, and promptly labeled the Northrop version the F-18L ("L" for land-based).

When the sales campaign was announced in June of 1976, Northrop chairman and CEO Thomas V. Jones was very careful not to step on the toes of his new partner. He stressed that the LBV was for export only, and that it would be substantially different from the F-18. The LBV was projected to be 7,000 pounds lighter than the carrier-based version, due to a lighter landing gear, simplified avionics package, elimination of a wing-fold, lighter arresting gear, and reduced internal fuel load. Jones also tip-toed around the Pentagon, noting that he had withdrawn his sales force from Europe as soon as the USAF-backed F-16 had been announced as the winner of the light-weight fighter competition and the likely choice of the European consortium of countries that would replace their F-104s with a new fighter. He attempted to impress the U.S. Congress by announcing that the export version would be funded completely from company funds, adding; "The defense industry should do its own financing for export products. We can't expect Congress to fund our plants and facilities for export items."

He could make an optimistic statement like that because his market studies had shown that the 100+ land-based air forces around the world would be in the market for an F-18-type airplane within the next few years. Northrop felt that this market would be at least 2,000 airplanes. The two-seat full scale mockup of the F-18L was unveiled in 1979, which was also the same year that Northrop and McDonnell began their six year legal battle over foreign sales of the Hornet.

Their disagreement had to do with aircraft sales to foreign countries. Northrop had entered into its agreement with McDonnell Douglas under the impression that all foreign sales would be theirs. McDonnell interpreted the agreement as giving Northrop all foreign sales of a land-based version of the Hornet. McDonnell was still interested in export sales of their carrier-capable F-18. While the two aerospace giants were ironing out their inter-company problems, they agreed to cooperate on sales of the Hornet to foreign countries, beginning with Canada.

The Canadian fighter force consisted of CF-101 Voodoo interceptors, CF-104 Starfighter air superiority fighters, and CF-5 Freedom

**The Canadian Air Force tested two CF-18s at the Aerospace Engineering Test Establishment, Cold Lake, ALberta during 1983. This CF-18 fires CRV7 2.75 inch rockets against a ground target in a test of rocket accuracy. (McDonnel Douglas)**

**Weapons tests were to verify flutter, performance, stability, control, separation, and jettison of various weapons loads. This CF-18B unloads six BL-755 cluster bombs while separation is filmed from cameras mounted under the wingtip. (McDonnell Douglas)**

**CF-18A (serial 188727) of 425 Squadron from CFB Bagotville, Canada deployed to Tyndall AFB, Florida in October of 86 for the 'William Tell 86' weapons exercise. This was the Hornet's first appearance at a William Tell competition. (Norman E. Taylor)**

Fighter lightweight fighters, all long in the tooth and ready for replacement. The idea of buying one airplane to replace all three was appealing, and was made more so by the sales incentives proposed by the two major competitors for this proposed $2.3 billion order. McDonnell Douglas offered up to $2.6 billion in "offsets", including 24,000 jobs, 8,000 of which were aerospace related. General Dynamics, in their CF-16 proposal, had offered $2.8 billion (later increased to $3.9 billion) in offsets. ("Offsets" are so-called because they are intended to offset the cost of procuring the aircraft. They can take the form of production of some of the parts of the aircraft in the customer's aircraft industry, government concessions on import-export restrictions, and price reductions based on the manufacturer writing off the cost of research and development). In the case of the Canadian sale, the offsets included such things as co-production of Canadian airplanes, a share in the production of other foreign versions, agreements to promote exports of other Canadian products, and efforts to encourage Canadian tourism.

Canadian military men were in favor of acquiring a twin-engine airplane to provide the extra margin of safety, and they made their point stick with the politicians. The announcement of the Canadian decision to buy the CF-18 was made in April of 1980. The contract was worth 2.34 billion Canadian dollars, and provided for offsets, 60% of which were in aerospace and electronics. It was expected that the program would provide 22,000 jobs over its fifteen year life cycle. Northrop got $450 million in subcontractor work. The program called for the acquisition of 137 Hornets (113 single-seaters, and 24 two-seaters). The CF-18 differed from the F/A-18 in the inclusion of a 600,000 candlepower spotlight on the left side of the forward fuselage, exchange of the water survival kit of the Navy version for a land-and-cold-weather survival kit, and exchange of the carrier landing instrument system for a land-base instrument landing system. Canadian CF-18 squadrons are; 410 Operational Training Squadron, 409 and 416 Squadrons at Cold Lake, Alberta, 425 and 434 Squadrons at Bagotville, Quebec, and the NATO contingent 439, 421, and 441 Squadrons at Baden Soellingen, Germany.

At the same time that McDonnell Douglas was wrapping up the Canadian contract a pair of Royal Australian Air Force pilots were visiting the United States to evaluate the F-16 and F-18. The Australians had announced their intention to buy seventy-five new fighters and had narrowed the choice to one of the lightweight fighter contenders. The twin engine configuration once again played a big part in their decision, with Australia announcing its intention to purchase seventy-five F-18s in October of 1981. Once again, the F-16 had lost out because of its single engine.

The Australians were reluctant to accept the risks inherent in the F-16's unproven all-weather targeting and navigation systems. And, even though the F-16s price was 7% less than that of the Hornet, the Australians figured that the difference would be more than offset in prevention of operational losses that would occur with a single-engined fighter. The larger size of the F/A-18 translated to a growth potential that was also an attractive incentive.

Once again, offsets played a major role in the contract award. The F-18 replacement of Australian Mirage III fighters was projected to cost $2.75 billion. Seventy-three of the seventy-five aircraft would undergo final assembly in Australia. 40% of the cost of the project was accounted for by offset work. This large share of Hornet production not only provided jobs in Australia, it was also responsible for the introduction of new technology to Australian industry. The technology transfer included titanium hot forming, titanium chemical milling and machining with five-axis machines, graphite-expoxy composite structure manufacture, radar production, aluminum no-draft precision forgings, and titanium forgings.

A strategic benefit to the United States from the Australian sale was having a country on the fringe of the vital Indian Ocean area operating the same aircraft as the U.S. Navy. This could translate into important logistical support in future operations.

There were similar reasons to support the Spanish purchase of seventy-two EF-18s, since both the USAF and US Navy use Spanish Air Force bases. The Spanish government conducted a study of available aircraft to replace a wide variety of aging types in the *Ejer-*

A pair of 425 Squadron Hornets patrol Canadian skies. The CF-18 replaces the CF-101 Voodoo, CF-104 Starfighter, and CF-5 Freedom Fighter in Canadian fighter squadrons. (McDonnell Douglas)

CF-18s of 409 'Nighthawk' Squadron enroute to the target range at CFB Cold Lake, Alberta. The squadron qualified at Cold Lake before deploying as part of the Canadian NATO contingent to Germany.

409 Squadron became operational at CFB Baden Soellingen, West Germany on 1 November 1985. The CF-18 replaced CF-104s expanding the duties of Canadian squadrons from air superiority to ground attack/air superiority. 409 Squadron was later joined by 439 and 421 Squadron. (McDonnell Douglas)

*cito del Aire*, and announced on 23 July 1982 that it had chosen the F-18. Spanish politics being what they are, there was a political flap immediately following the announcement concerning a $50,000 agent's fee that had been paid to *Compania Aeronautica Espanola, S.A.* of Madrid. McDonnell Douglas was also using Antonio Garrigues Walker, leader of the Liberal Democratic Party, as its attorney in Spain. The Socialists, in that year's political campaign, promised to get rid of the F-18 if elected, but when they were elected, they signed a letter of acceptance for the F-18s on 31 May 1983!

CF-18A (serial 188724) of 410 Squadron based at CFB Cold Lake, Alberta on the ramp at McChord AFB, Washington on 22 March 1986. Canadian aircraft are common visitors at USAF bases. (Douglas Remington via Norm Taylor)

F/A-18Bs of Number 2 Operational Conversion Unit (OCU) Royal Australian Air Force (RAAF) on the ramp at Williamtown, New South Wales. No. 2 OCU trains Hornet pilots for all operational RAAF squadrons. (McDonnell Douglas)

(Above) CF-18A (serial 188106) reveals the false canopy painted on the undersides of all Canadian Hornets. In a turning fight, the false canopy might convince an enemy pilot that the Hornet is turning into him when it is actually turning away. (via Norm Taylor)

(Below) An F/A-18B of 2 OCU over the Pacific. The first three RAAF Hornets were manufactured in St. Louis, however, the balance of the initial order of seventy-five aircraft will be assembled in Australia. (McDonnell Douglas)

F/A-18Bs of 2 OCU taxi out for another mission. Australia has projected a 6,000 hour airframe life and an average annual use of 300 hours. With this projected life it is a safe bet that the Hornet will remain in service into the 21st Century. (McDonnell Douglas)

An RAAF F/A-18A with the flaps set at maneuvering position. The RAAF plans to have three Hornet squadrons operational, with the balance of the F/A-18s in a replacement pool. Two squadrons are to be based at Williamtown, with the third at Tindal in the Northern Territories. (McDonnell Douglas)

The first of seventy-two EF-18 Hornets for the Spanish Air Force during assembly at the McDonnell plant in St. Louis. This aircraft was rolled out during November of 1985.

The first three EF-18 Hornets for the Spanish Air force were delivered to Spain in early Summer of 1986. Spanish pilots receive conversion training in the Hornet at Whitman AFB before returning home to join an operational squadron. (McDonnell Douglas)

# Modern Military Aircraft

## by Lou Drendel

**5001**

**5002**

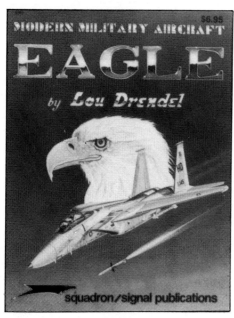

**5003**

**5004**

# squadron/signal publications, inc.